Cinnamon grey green

Other titles of interest:

The Tropical Aquarium
Community Fishes
Marine Fishes
Maintaining a Healthy Aquarium
Aquarium Plants
Central American Cichlids
Fish Breeding
African and Asian Catfishes
South American Catfishes
Koi
Livebearing Fishes
Fancy Goldfishes
Reptiles and Amphibians
Hamsters, Gerbils, Rats, Mice and Chinchillas
Rabbits and Guinea Pigs
Pet Birds
Softbills
Finches

A Birdkeeper's Guide to

Budgies

Lacewing yellow and yellow-wing dark green

Photographs by Cyril Laubscher

Greywing cobalt and greywing light green

A Birdkeeper's Guide to

Budgies

An invaluable guide for both beginners and enthusiasts
on keeping and breeding these popular birds

David Alderton

Tetra⬦Press

16087

A Salamander Book

© 1988, 1997 Salamander Books Ltd.,
Published in the USA by Tetra Press,
3001 Commerce Street,
Blacksburg, VA 24060.

ISBN 1 56465 152 5

This (revised) edition © 1997 Salamander Books Ltd.

Normal sky blue

Credits

Editor: Anne McDowall   Design: Jill Coote
Color reproductions:
Contemporary Lithoplates Ltd..
Filmset: SX Composing DTP
Printed in China

Author

David Alderton has kept and bred a wide variety of birds for more than thirty years. He has travelled extensively in pursuit of this interest, visiting other enthusiasts in various parts of the world, including the United States, Canada and Australia, where he observed some of the first examples of the now popular spangle mutation. He has previously written a number of books on avicultural subjects, and contributes regularly to general and specialist publications in the UK and overseas. David studied veterinary medicine at Cambridge University, and now, in addition to writing, runs a highly respected international service that offers advice on the needs of animals kept in both domestic and commercial environments. He is also a Council Member of the Avicultural Society.

Photographer

Cyril Laubscher has been interested in aviculture and ornithology for more than forty years and has travelled extensively in Europe, Australia and Southern Africa photographing wildlife. When he left England for Australia in 1966 as an enthusiastic aviculturalist, this fascination found expression as he began to portray birds photographically. In Australia he met the well-known aviculturalist Stan Sindel and, as a result of this association, seventeen of Cyril's photographs were published in Joseph Forshaw's original book on Australian Parrots in 1969. Since then, his photographs have met with considerable acclaim and the majority of those that appear here were taken specially for this book.

Contents

Introduction

The Budgerigar was first brought to Europe by the explorer and naturalist John Gould, in 1840, and soon achieved considerable popularity. Indeed, within forty years, commercial breeding establishments, accommodating over 100,000 birds, were supplying a growing demand for budgerigars in Europe. Colour mutations started to emerge towards the end of the nineteenth century which reinforced the appeal of the budgerigar; new colours were a novelty, and represented considerable financial gain for breeders lucky enough to produce such birds. Public shows, coupled with the formation of the Budgerigar Club (later renamed the Budgerigar Society) in Britain in 1925, brought these parakeets and the new colours to an even wider audience and the budgerigar soon began to overtake the canary in popularity. Today, it is the most widely-kept companion bird in the world, with millions being kept as pet, aviary and exhibition subjects.

Budgerigars are highly adaptable birds, occurring naturally in arid and often inhospitable terrain in Australia. They are easy to keep and undemanding in their feeding habits, even when breeding. Unlike many other members of the parrot family, they are not noisy birds, yet they are mimics, able to reproduce the sounds of human speech, and their lively and naturally tame personalities have endeared them to pet-owners of all ages. While they may give a painful nip if handled carelessly, budgerigars are not difficult to restrain when necessary, and are safe for children to handle. Furthermore, unlike other Australian parakeets, they settle well in a cage and can live for eight years or more.

Whether you are seeking a bird as a companion, or thinking of setting up a garden aviary, you will find that keeping budgerigars is a relaxing and rewarding hobby. You may even decide to start exhibiting budgerigars as your interest grows!

Choosing a budgerigar

Whether you are looking for a pet or for aviary or exhibition stock, there are certain things you will need to look for in a budgerigar. You will want to know the age of a bird and its sex, particularly if you are intending to keep two or more birds together. More importantly, you will need to ensure that the budgerigar you select is healthy. In this section we discuss how to choose healthy and suitable budgerigars as pets for the home or as aviary subjects.

Sexing budgerigars
Budgerigars are sexed by the colour of the cere, which is the fleshy area containing the nostrils just above the beak. Adult hens invariably have brown ceres, whereas the ceres of cocks are normally bluish. (In a few cases, notably the recessive pied group and both the lutino and albino varieties, the cere of cock birds will remain a pinkish purple colour).

You may have difficulty in sexing young budgerigars, as this distinction is less obvious in juveniles. It will help if there are a number of chicks available for you to compare. However, young cocks do have slightly more prominent and usually darker, more purplish ceres than females. As the budgerigars mature, this difference in cere colour becomes more distinct.

Traditionally, it has been accepted that cock birds make the best pets, proving more talented talkers than their female counterparts. These observations may be true to a certain extent, but hens can prove quite reliable mimics and are great characters. There appears to be no difference between the different colour varieties in terms of their talking abilities, although dominant pieds often prove less nervous than their

Below: *If you are looking for a budgerigar as a pet, be sure to choose a young bird. Eyes, cere and markings should all provide an indication of its immaturity.*

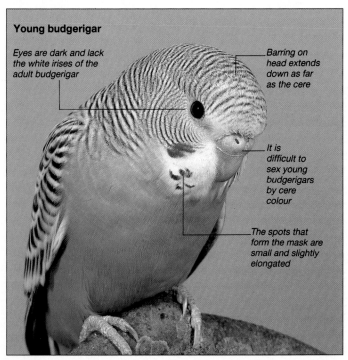

Young budgerigar

Eyes are dark and lack the white irises of the adult budgerigar

Barring on head extends down as far as the cere

It is difficult to sex young budgerigars by cere colour

The spots that form the mask are small and slightly elongated

recessive counterparts, and may be easier to tame as a result.

Choosing a young bird

In most cases, it is best to buy a young budgerigar. This will probably be cheaper than an adult bird and certainly should be easier to tame; budgerigars that have recently left the nest should sit quite readily on a finger extended parallel with the perch, provided they have not been disturbed.

Apart from the basic distinction in cere coloration, a number of other features can be significant when assessing the relative youth of a budgerigar. Look firstly at the eyes, which should be solid and dark in a young bird, showing no trace of the white irises that will appear around the perimeter in an adult bird. These start to become

Below: *Compare this mature normal cobalt with the young bird shown opposite. The age of an adult can be determined only if it is wearing a closed ring.*

evident only when the youngster is approaching 12 weeks of age.

The head markings of a young bird are also distinctive, especially in the so-called 'normal varieties'. The darker wavy pattern of banding in the plumage extending up to the cere and the barred pattern on the forehead have given rise to the name of 'barhead' for young budgerigars. This pattern is lost at the first moult, and is replaced by clear plumage.

You should also be able to see the spots that form the so-called 'mask' on the head. These are relatively thin and slightly elongated in youngsters, but become much more prominent in older budgerigars. In some of the lighter coloured varieties, including lutino and recessive pieds, however, this distinction may not be apparent, because of the total or partial lack of the dark pigment melanin (see page 80).

Although legs that appear heavily scaled will indicate an old budgerigar it is virtually impossible

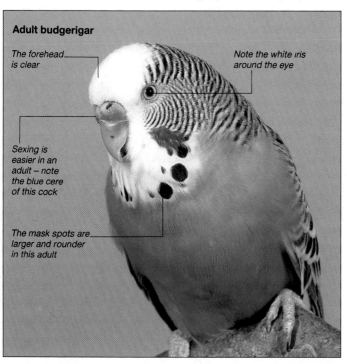

Adult budgerigar

The forehead is clear

Note the white iris around the eye

Sexing is easier in an adult – note the blue cere of this cock

The mask spots are larger and rounder in this adult

to age an adult budgerigar accurately and usually you will have to rely on the vendor's honesty. However, if you are buying from a breeder, the birds may be ringed. Closed rings, which can be fitted only to young birds in the nest, provide a reliable indicator of the budgerigar's age. These rings are marked with the year of hatching and may also carry a sequential number, the breeder's initials and club details. Split rings, however, are used more for identification purposes. One way of ensuring that you have birds of known age is to purchase current-year budgerigars, which should be ready to nest during the following year.

Choosing a healthy bird
Naturally, you will want to buy a healthy bird, and many of the signs of ill health are clearly visible if you know what to look for. Choose an individual that is lively and plump. You can assess the bird's weight by feeling the breastbone, down the centre of the lower part of the body. This should be well covered with muscle, with no distinct gaps on either side of the bone.

Check the wings for signs of French moult, a viral condition which results in the loss of flight feathers and sometimes tail feathers in young budgerigars. In a mild case, these may regrow; often, a badly affected budgerigar may never be able to fly properly. This might not be a handicap in a pet bird; in fact, you may prefer to have a budgerigar whose flight is handicapped, so that it will be easier to catch when at liberty in the room and there is no risk of the bird escaping.

However, the moulting period can bring on additional problems. In a budgerigar suffering from French moult, the new flight feathers can prove brittle and may break at their bases. As the feathers are still receiving a blood supply at this stage – clear from the reddish tips at the end of the feathers nearest to the wing – this can lead to bleeding. If you have a

budgerigar afflicted with French moult, always have a styptic pencil available, so that you can stop any blood loss without delay.

If you are buying adult stock, you will find it more difficult to spot the effects of this virus. Where a budgerigar has been afflicted with a mild case of French moult as a youngster, the flight and tail feathers will have regrown and the symptoms will be virtually undetectable in the adult bird. Open the wing and look closely a short distance along from the bases of the primary flight feathers. In a healthy bird, the shaft should appear clear. If there is a reddish brown area along the shaft, this shows that the budgerigar was almost certainly affected with French moult earlier in life. The tail feathers may show similar symptoms. Since this disease is caused by a virus, for which there is presently no cure, avoid buying such birds as they could infect chicks in due course.

Below: *This budgerigar is suffering from the feather disease, French moult. Symptoms first appear in young birds and vary in severity.*

Another point to check for in young budgerigars is the shape of the beak. Under normal circumstances, the upper part of the beak should overlap the lower part. In some cases, however, the beak can become undershot, with the upper mandible failing to make contact with the lower and curling round inside the bill, under the tongue. The lower part of the beak will then start to grow excessively and will need to be cut back regularly with a stout pair of clippers. Although this problem may be of genetic origin in some cases, dirty nesting conditions are often the cause - droppings stuck under the tongue, at the front of the lower beak, can be responsible. The upper mandible may also be malformed for the same reason, but this is less common. Check the beaks of young budgerigars periodically and remove any accumulated food. Unfortunately, by the time that an affected chick leaves the nest, nothing can be done to deal with the problem, apart from regular

Above: *Note how the upper beak has curved inside the lower in this budgerigar. Regular cutting back with clippers will be required.*

clipping to ensure that the budgerigar can continue eating without difficulty. If you do not feel able to undertake this task, it is probably best to avoid purchasing such a bird.

When you open the wings, you may see feather lice – relatively long, thin parasites – running parallel with the contour of the feathers, at right angles to the feather shaft. These parasites are less mobile than mites, and can be killed with the same treatment (see page 17). One type of mite not usually obvious on young budgerigars is *Cnemidocoptes*, responsible for the condition described as scaly face. These parasites tend to localize around the beak, and often on the legs as well. Look closely for any trace of snail-like tracks across the upper beak, which is an early sign of this disease. In more advanced cases,

15

coral-like encrustations around the sides of the beak may be apparent. These can spread around the cere and even over the body. The legs may show similar signs. Scaly face can lead to malformation of the beak, but in a mild case treatment is straightforward and the budgerigar will not suffer permanent disfigurement.

Buying a pet budgerigar

The majority of people who keep a budgerigar in the home prefer a single pet bird to a pair or small colony. Certainly, a budgerigar housed on its own is likely to prove a better companion, but if two youngsters are obtained together and trained as individuals, both can become very tame and will mimic their owner. If you do decide to keep two birds together, two cocks will present fewer difficulties than a pair and are unlikely to be as quarrelsome as two hens.

You will need to obtain a recently fledged budgerigar about six weeks old. At this stage it will be ready to be moved to its new home. It is easier to find suitable budgerigars in the summer and early autumn, since keepers who breed their birds in outside aviaries on a colony system will have stock available then. There is no need to obtain a chick from an exhibition breeder; such budgerigars tend to be relatively costly, and their lifespan may well prove shorter than that of smaller and less illustrious stock. A local pet store or bird farm may have a good choice of baby budgies available. Alternatively, contact a breeder via the advertisement columns of a local newspaper or seek out your nearest cage bird society. You can find details at your library or in the pages of specialist birdkeeping publications. Most budgerigar breeders will be willing to help you choose a suitable pet.

Buying aviary budgerigars

Budgerigars make lively aviary occupants but, because of their destructive nature, they will

Above: *This bird is suffering from scaly face, caused by a parasitical infestation. If left untreated, the beak will become malformed.*

destroy any plants in the enclosure and are therefore best kept in a relatively sparse flight. Although budgerigars will live peacefully together in a group, it is best not to mix them with other birds; they may attack other birds or spoil their breeding attempts. The Cockatiel (*Nymphicus hollandicus*) sometimes proves a suitable companion, and larger finches, such as weavers and Java sparrows (*Lonchura oryzivora*), are occasionally kept with budgerigars, but be aware of the potential problems likely to occur, especially when the birds are breeding; the budgerigars may interfere with the efforts of their companions. If you would like to include budgerigars in a mixed aviary, cock birds on their own tend to be less aggressive than hens. Small numbers of budgerigars are generally more amenable towards other birds than are a large flock.

If you are planning on setting up an exhibition stud of budgerigars, then you will need to visit a suitable breeder. Aviary stock is more widely available and considerably cheaper, because there is far less investment required in budgerigars of this type. You may be able to purchase the complete stock of someone who is selling up, usually at a competitive price, but this means that you will have to take all their birds. Alternatively, you can buy odd individuals and pairs from different sources. This allows you to choose only those budgerigars that appeal to you.

However, obtaining birds in this way does heighten the risk of introducing disease or parasites to budgerigars obtained from other suppliers. It is therefore advisable to house all new arrivals separately for at least a fortnight. Watch them closely to check their health, and treat them with an aerosol preparation to kill mites and lice, specially marketed for use with birds. Two applications, at an interval of a fortnight, are usually recommended. Although this may seem a troublesome and rather unnecessary precaution, it is considerably easier to deal with a potential health problem at this stage, rather than once the birds are all together in the aviary. Red mites can be introduced to an aviary by an infected bird and they can become a major problem, especially during the breeding period. They tend to localize in dark areas, such as nestboxes.

Bringing the bird home
Special cardboard carrying boxes, suitable for young budgerigars, are supplied by most pet stores, but if you are buying a bird from a breeder, you should check first whether you need to take a container with you. A shoe box lined with newspaper and with ventilation holes punched in the sides will be adequate, but be sure to secure the lid in place with string or tape, to prevent the budgerigar escaping.

Prepare the cage or aviary before releasing the budgerigar inside. Ensure that all equipment is in position and that there is an adequate supply of food and water. This will enable the bird to settle into its new surroundings with a minimum of disturbance. It is always advisable to wash a cage, even when it is not contaminated in any way. Never use very hot water or anti-parasitic aerosol sprays on the plastic base of a cage as they may discolour it. Encourage aviary birds to use the shelter; it may be worth shutting them in for a few days before allowing them out into the flight.

Below: *Use a cardboard box rather than a cage for moving a budgie. Remember to provide ventilation holes and secure the lid with tape.*

Housing budgerigars in the home

There are many different designs of cages available that are suitable for budgerigars. The traditional bird cage is formed entirely of wire mesh, whereas a breeding cage is usually in the form of a box, with solid walls and a wire mesh front. In this section we discuss vital points to consider when selecting a cage for a pet budgerigar, including the most appropriate types of perches and floor coverings. Later in the section, we look at how to build a box cage and an indoor flight.

The bird cage
You can easily obtain a cage for a pet budgerigar from your local pet store. If possible, however, visit one of the larger outlets first, to see a wider selection of the types available. Choose a design which will allow the budgerigar as much flying space as possible, since you may not always be able to let your pet out into the room. Rectangular cages are therefore preferable to vertical or circular designs.

The colour of the bars is not really significant and although a silver-type finish is traditional, a much wider range of colours is now available. Avoid a cage which shows signs of damage, such as a chipped coating, however, since rust may develop and spoil the appearance of the cage as well as

pose a potential health hazard to the budgerigar. Some designs have bars covered with a white epoxy resin to prolong the lifespan of the cage and facilitate cleaning; you can easily wipe any dirt or droppings from this surface with a damp paper towel.

Older cages tend to incorporate more wire mesh in their design, and the lower sides are enclosed with lengths of glass or plastic to prevent seed husks being scattered into the room. These cages are potentially more difficult to clean, but, if treated carefully, should prove as durable as more modern designs. The cage which you choose should last for the whole of your budgerigar's life.

Door fastenings are a weakness in the design of some cages; doors that swing shut on their own may harm the budgerigar if it attempts to escape as you close the door. Choose a cage which has a clip to hold the door closed, in preference to one with a spring.

Depending on where you decide to position the cage in the home, you may want to obtain a stand for it. However, stability is vital; young children (or pets, such as dogs)

Below: Choose a spacious cage for your budgie. You may want a stand, and a cover to fit around the base to catch seed husks.

Fitting perches in the cage

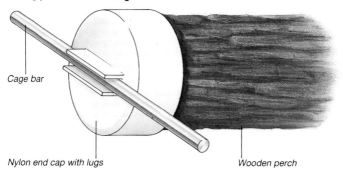

Cage bar

Nylon end cap with lugs

Wooden perch

can bump into the stand. Clearly, if it is knocked over, then both the bird and child may be hurt. It may well be better, therefore, to position the cage on furniture rather than use a stand.

Perches
Most cages are supplied complete with perches. If these are of plastic, replace them straight away. The trend towards plastic rather than wooden dowelling perches can perhaps be justified on grounds of hygiene, but plastic perches are simply not comfortable for most budgerigars; birds in cages with plastic perches usually prefer to cling to the sides of their cage.

Wooden dowelling is commonly used for perches; 12.5mm(0.5in) diameter is best for budgerigars as it is narrow enough for the birds to grip easily yet wide enough to prevent their claws touching underneath the perch. The main disadvantage with dowelling is that it is of a constant diameter and, over a period of time, the parts of the bird's feet which are more in contact with the dowelling than others are likely to develop into pronounced pressure points, particularly in obese budgerigars. Apart from causing discomfort, these can also be a focus of infection, which may develop into bumblefoot, a condition best recognized in birds of prey.

The best material for perches is natural wood. Branches can be cut

Above: *These plastic ends enable you to attach perches easily and directly to the sides of the cage, without having to distort the bars.*

from a variety of trees – sycamore and apple are particularly good. Natural branches, being of variable diameter, enable the budgerigar to alter its grip, thus preventing the development of pressure sores. You will probably be able to fit only two perches in the cage, as you will need to ensure that they do not overhang seed and water containers. Cut the branches so that they fit comfortably within the cage, and avoid distorting the bars. Ideally, the perches should extend in a virtually straight line across the cage. If they are crowded at either end, the budgerigar's tail may rub repeatedly on the bars and cause its feathers to become frayed.

Budgerigars will be able to gnaw at the natural wood perches, thus helping to prevent their beaks becoming overgrown. It is significant that budgerigars living in aviaries where wooden perches are always supplied invariably prove far less prone to overgrown beaks than their pet counterparts kept in cages without natural branches. You may be able to use the tips normally fitted to dowel perches, which slot into the bars of the cage, to hold natural branches in place. Alternatively, you can cut a notch directly into the wood, so that it fits in a similar way, without distorting the bars. Some cages are also equipped with a swing, and your bird may use this regularly. If the swing is ignored, however, remove it and replace it with a higher perch; budgerigars tend to seek out the highest site to perch as darkness falls.

Cleaning and floor coverings
Cleanliness is obviously important, and a cage with a detachable base will be much easier to clean. Most of the dirt will accumulate on the floor of the cage, and if you can remove the base then washing the floor regularly will be an easier task. Avoid clear plastic bases, however, because scratches will soon show and young budgerigars, in particular, may run up and down the sides of the cage in an attempt to find an exit, failing to appreciate the presence of this plastic barrier in their path.

Sandsheets are an ideal way to line the floor of the cage and are available in various sizes to fit most standard cages. They are easy to change and tend to be less messy than loose bird sand; you can simply scrape off the droppings every day, and replace the sheet itself once or twice a week. This will ensure that the cage remains clean, and that scattering of seed and feathers into the room is minimal. Some adult hen budgerigars in breeding condition have a tendency to chew sandsheets, however.

Sand has the advantage of being relatively cheap and may provide useful grit and minerals, but it is heavy to carry and it does not give such a good covering as a sandsheet. You will probably need to replace a thick layer of sand on the floor of the cage each day and you may have to wash the tray every time you clean the cage. It is inadvisable to use sand for cages housing laying hens as they have a tendency to scratch around the floor and the sand may become introduced into the vent and cause considerable irritation. Newspaper is a cheap and practical alternative but is unsightly. As a compromise,

you can camouflage it with a light sprinkling of sand.

Irrespective of whether or not you choose a stand, it is useful to fit a flexible plastic cover around the base of the cage to help prevent seed husks and feathers from being scattered in the room. Budgerigars are likely to produce a certain amount of dust, particularly when moulting, which will settle around the cage. If the cage is on a flat surface, you can wipe this up easily each day with a damp cloth.

The box cage
Cages of this type are rarely seen in the home, but are quite suitable for housing a pet bird. Indeed, they provide more flying space and are ideal if you have enough room to accommodate one and cannot let your bird out of its cage to exercise. In the birdroom (see page 36), these cages are used for housing breeding budgerigars and for holding stock on a temporary basis. Either obtain a ready-built cage, or buy the front separately and build your own cage around it. If you are building a cage of this type for a pet bird, then opt for one long front, rather than two smaller ones; this will be easier to fit and looks more attractive. For a budgerigar, the length of the front should be about 90cm(36in). The height of the front is less significant; 38cm(15in) will be adequate. This will give an overall cage height of about 45cm(18in), allowing for a wooden support of 1.25cm(0.5in) at the top and bottom of the front, and a gap of about 2.5cm(1in) for a sliding tray on the floor of the cage. It should be at least 38cm(15in) front to back.

While the dimensions may not be very significant for a cage in the home, they will be important when planning the layout of a birdroom. Build the box with 6mm(0.25in) plywood. Some breeders prefer to use hardboard instead of plywood as it is cheaper and easier to cut, leaving cleaner edges. Unfortunately, it is less durable, and warps more easily, especially when it is washed.

Above: *Box cages offer a versatile means of housing budgerigars. Here, the centre partition is being removed, doubling the flight area.*

Ideally, order the component pieces already cut to size so that you can simply assemble them to form the box unit. You may not need to build a wooden framework; you should be able to tack the individual pieces together with small screws or panel pins. Avoid glue, as it may prove toxic if consumed by the budgerigars. Ensure that the various components fit together well, and that there are no loose edges which the budgerigars can gnaw.

Before assembling the panels, paint the interior of the cage with a light-coloured emulsion. You may need two or three coats to give an adequate covering, depending upon the material you have used. Paint the exterior in a darker contrasting colour, if you wish.

You will find it relatively easy to convert a box cage of this type into a breeding cage at a later date. Do this by incorporating two fronts into one relatively large cage and placing a removable partition between them to form a double breeding cage. In this type of cage, young birds can be separated in one half, while their

parents rear a second round of chicks on the other side of the partition. A standard budgerigar cage is less satisfactory for breeding purposes, partly because it is difficult to fix a nestbox to such a cage.

The indoor flight
Another option worth considering for housing two pairs of breeding budgerigars together is an indoor flight. You can buy small indoor aviaries suitable for this purpose from specialist manufacturers, and some firms will build a suitable structure to your own design. Alternatively, you may prefer to construct one yourself. A flight 180cm(6ft) high and 90cm(3ft) wide and deep should be adequate. Like the box cage, it should have solid plywood sides. These will help to restrict the scattering of seed husks and other debris into the room where the budgies are kept. In addition, it will be easier to attach nestboxes to the sides of the flight for the breeding period. Again, you will need a sliding tray on the floor of the enclosure.

Construct a frame for the front of the unit using 1.25cm(0.5in) square wood, to fit snugly within the interior of the box. You can buy the wire mesh for the front of the flight from various outlets, including DIY stores and garden centres. It is available in various thicknesses; for budgerigars, 19 gauge (19G) is the most suitable grade as it is sufficiently durable, but cheaper than thicker 16G mesh. The size of the mesh is also significant; 2.5cmx1.25cm (1x0.5in) will be fine. You can use so-called chicken wire, but it is difficult to cut without leaving sharp edges. Square or rectangular mesh, on the other hand, is very easy to cut and you can file back any slight projections as necessary.

Cut the mesh with sharp pliers or wire-cutters and use netting staples to fix it to the inner surface of the wooden frame that will form the front of the flight cage. This will protect the woodwork from the budgerigars' beaks. Carry out this stage of the construction process on a flat surface to ensure that the mesh is kept both square and taut on the frame, otherwise the flight's appearance will be spoiled.

Start by tacking both top corners in place, keeping the mesh parallel with the corresponding edge of the framework. Then move along each side, pulling the mesh down before fixing the staples in place. Check that the sides are parallel and, finally, fix the bottom edge of the mesh in place, trimming off any surplus. You will need to make a small door, approximately 15cm(6in) square, so that you can replenish the budgerigars' food and sweep out any husks which may have accumulated behind the sliding tray. This should be located about 45cm(18in) from the base of the flight cage and can be fitted either in the front mesh or at either end, in the plywood panels. If you fit the door in the front mesh then you will need to cut around the opening and fix the loose edges to the door frame. You can then fit the cut section over the door itself. Hinge the door at the lower edge of the frame so that it opens downwards and outwards. This will enable you to reach inside the cage without difficulty. Keep the door closed with small bolts or hasps. It is a

good idea to make a door in one side as well, large enough to give you easy access to the nestboxes when necessary. Be careful when opening this side door, however, as the budgerigars may try to escape into the room. The smaller doors are therefore important for routine daily care.

Use battening to cover any sharp ends of wire which could prove especially hazardous for budgerigars wearing rings of any type – the bird could become caught in the mesh if a strand becomes lodged underneath the ring. Budgerigars are especially vulnerable in this respect as they often spend quite long periods climbing on the mesh of their

The indoor flight

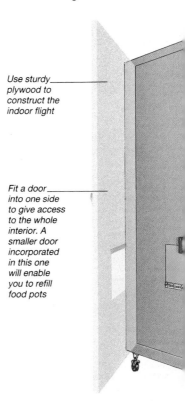

Use sturdy plywood to construct the indoor flight

Fit a door into one side to give access to the whole interior. A smaller door incorporated in this one will enable you to refill food pots

Mount the flight on castors to enable you to move it easily

quarters. Choose a hardwood battening if possible because, although it is expensive, it will be far more durable than softer battening, which the birds can easily destroy with their beaks. Use strips 1.25cm(0.5in) wide and 6mm(0.25in) thick. Having cut them to the appropriate length, tack them in place over the cut ends of wire with narrow-headed panel pins. Do not paint the battening, because the budgerigars will inevitably gnaw at the wood and the appearance of the interior of the flight will be spoiled. Damage to natural wood will be less evident.

A sheet of plastic or plywood fixed across the front of the flight and extending about 30cm(12in) above the opening for the tray will help to prevent seed husks being scattered around the room. This covering will be largely protected by the wire mesh, but to ensure that it is fully out of reach of the budgerigars, it is a good idea to mount it on a framework of 1.25cm(0.5in) square wood.

While you may want to keep the flight in one room, it can be useful mount it on castors so that you can easily move it to clean behind it. You can buy these castors from a hardware store and either screw them directly onto the base or fix them onto wooden blocks which you can then glue to the bottom of the flight cage.

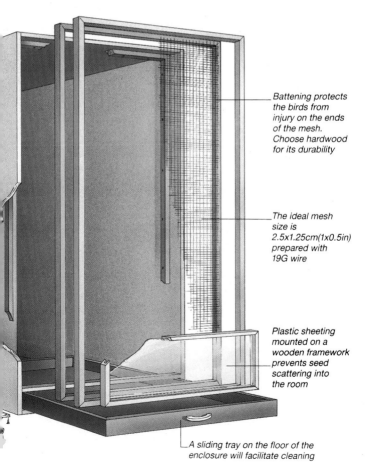

Battening protects the birds from injury on the ends of the mesh. Choose hardwood for its durability

The ideal mesh size is 2.5x1.25cm(1x0.5in) prepared with 19G wire

Plastic sheeting mounted on a wooden framework prevents seed scattering into the room

A sliding tray on the floor of the enclosure will facilitate cleaning

Housing budgerigars in the garden

Budgerigars are hardy birds, and will live quite happily throughout the year in an outside aviary. They do need protection from the elements however, and for this reason the aviary is typically divided into two sections. The outer unit, a wooden-framed wire structure, is known as the flight, and the closed in shed-like part is usually referred to as the shelter. Exhibition budgerigar breeders, in particular, often incorporate the shelter into a larger structure, known as a birdroom. This provides more space for breeding and training stock.

Obtaining a basic aviary for budgerigars is relatively straightforward, as a number of firms now produce aviaries in kit form. The component parts, which are often pre-drilled to facilitate assembly, can be delivered to your door. Nevertheless, it is worthwhile visiting manufacturers in your area before placing a definite order. The quality of aviaries on offer varies, and you may not always get what you pay for! Check, in particular, whether or not extras, such as treatment of the woodwork with a suitable preservative, are included in the basic price.

Demand for aviaries is, not surprisingly, at its highest during the spring and summer months. Manufacturers will often clear display models towards the end of the year and you may well be able to obtain a bargain then. It can be difficult to erect an aviary once the risk of frost is present, however; you will need to prepare solid foundations for the structure and frost will interfere with the laying of concrete and mortar, so avoid building this stage in cold weather.

Siting the aviary
Plan the location of the aviary in advance, allowing for the possibility of expansion later. Ideally, choose a well-drained, sheltered area, out of the prevailing wind. However, if necessary, you can plant a row of fast-growing conifers to provide protection from the wind.

Preparing the foundations will be easier if the site is reasonably level. As far as possible, conceal the structure from the front of the house; budgerigars may provide a target for passing vandals and sitting hens are likely to be disturbed by car headlamps after dark. Disturbances of this sort may result in losses of eggs and chicks. Avoid, too, siting the aviary in a position where it could cause difficulties with neighbours, such as next to the garden fence adjoining their home. Although the chatter of budgerigars is not usually disturbing, it could cause offence early in the morning if the aviary directly adjoins a bedroom window. You may even need to apply for official permission to construct an aviary, depending on local regulations. Check with the relevant authorities that you have the necessary planning permission before you begin work.

Preparing the site
Mark out the chosen area with canes and then carefully cut out any turf within these boundaries. You may wish to transfer this turf to a shady part of the garden and, provided that you keep it moistened, you can use it to fill in damaged areas at a later date.

The next stage will be to prepare the footings for the aviary. You will need to dig out soil around the perimeter of the area to make a trench 45cm(18in) deep, in which to lay the blocks that will ultimately support the aviary framework. Excavate the trench slightly wider than the blocks so that you can position them with greater ease on a bed of mortar. Depending on the soil conditions, you may also need shuttering, to prevent earth falling onto the blockwork until this is set fast in position. Boards of the appropriate length, held in place by pegs driven into the floor of the trench, will serve this purpose and can be removed easily at a later date. If necessary, compress a layer of rubble behind the blockwork once it is fixed in place and transfer the soil elsewhere.

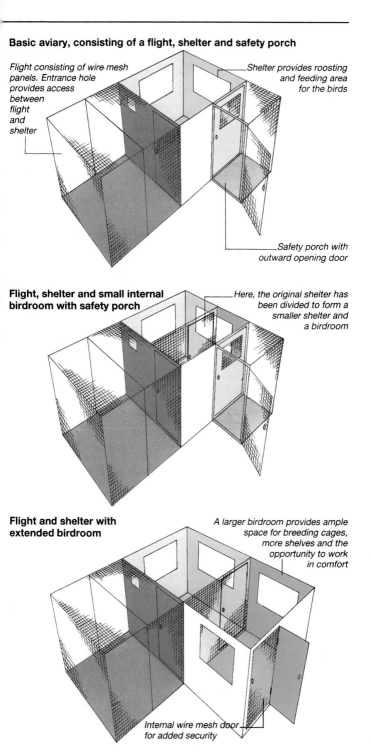

Basic aviary, consisting of a flight, shelter and safety porch

Flight consisting of wire mesh panels. Entrance hole provides access between flight and shelter

Shelter provides roosting and feeding area for the birds

Safety porch with outward opening door

Flight, shelter and small internal birdroom with safety porch

Here, the original shelter has been divided to form a smaller shelter and a birdroom

Flight and shelter with extended birdroom

A larger birdroom provides ample space for breeding cages, more shelves and the opportunity to work in comfort

Internal wire mesh door for added security

25

The floor of the aviary

At this stage it is important that you decide on the type of floor you want in the aviary. While a concrete base is usual in the shelter, a grass floor may be adequate for the flight. However, although this may sound a more attractive option than concrete, paving slabs or gravel, it will not prove so satisfactory in the long run. The grass will tend to die back, especially as the budgerigars will eat it, and drainage may prove a problem, giving rise to muddy patches during wet weather. The surface will also be very difficult to clean, and this will put the budgerigars at risk from enteric diseases.

Preparing a concrete floor requires the excavation of more soil and, since much of this is likely to be subsoil of little horticultural value, you may prefer to dispose of it in a skip, rather than incorporating it in the existing garden landscape. Excavate the floor area to an approximate depth of 23cm(9in) and fill to about 15cm(6in) with a well-compacted layer of hardcore. You may wish to hire a small concrete mixer to prepare the concrete for the floor covering, as this can be an arduous and time-consuming task.

A coarse mix – three parts ballast to one part cement powder – will be good enough for the initial foundations. It is easier to work the ingredients together while they are still relatively dry, and then add the water in small amounts. If you are preparing the concrete by hand, mix it well with a spade and add water gradually, so that you do not make it too wet and sloppy. If you can hire a mixer, you will need simply to place the appropriate quantities in the machine. Depending on the accessibility of the site, it may be worth ordering ready-mixed cement. Do not worry too much about the finish; simply smooth the mix over the foundations as evenly as possible.

The top layer, which should consist of equal measures of sand and cement, will need to be

Preparing the site

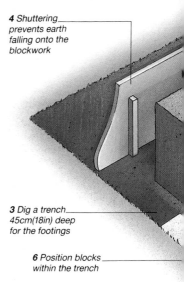

8 Excavate the floor area to a depth of approx. 23cm(9in)

4 Shuttering prevents earth falling onto the blockwork

3 Dig a trench 45cm(18in) deep for the footings

6 Position blocks within the trench

9 Fill this floor area with approx. 15cm(6in) of well-compacted hardcore

prepared more carefully and you may wish to hire a plasterer to do this part of the job to ensure a smooth, even finish to the aviary floor. If it is carried out badly, water will not drain off properly and will accumulate in puddles. The floor should slope to a drainage hole situated at the end of the aviary furthest from the shelter. During a heavy storm, however, this drainage hole may become blocked by feathers, and 2.5cm(1in) of water accumulating here will be enough to saturate any budgerigar which lands in it. Two small drainage holes rather than

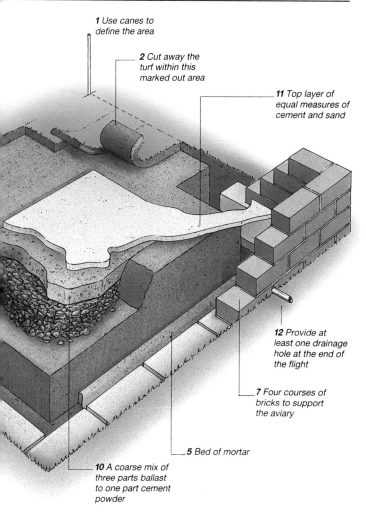

1 Use canes to define the area

2 Cut away the turf within this marked out area

11 Top layer of equal measures of cement and sand

12 Provide at least one drainage hole at the end of the flight

7 Four courses of bricks to support the aviary

5 Bed of mortar

10 A coarse mix of three parts ballast to one part cement powder

one, will lessen the risk of such flooding occurring.

The cement mixture must not be too sandy or the surface will become flaky, and you may find unsightly algal growth on the floor during periods of wet weather. Allowing it to dry out too quickly can lead to similar problems. If the weather is very warm, cover the damp mortar with hessian sacking or similar material to protect the vulnerable surface. It may well take a couple of days for the base to dry thoroughly, and you will need to keep cats and other animals off the area during this time! If

possible, therefore, lay flight panels on top of the footings, to cover the whole floor without coming into direct contact with drying cement.

Paving slabs are a more temporary alternative to a concrete base, since they can be removed from the site more easily. However, they must be set on a firm surface, so, again, you will need to prepare a bed of hardcore. Place a layer of mortar on top of the hardcore to anchor the slabs as they are fixed in position. Depending on the floor area, you may need to cut the paving slabs

27

to fit around the perimeter of the aviary floor; use a chisel to create a line of weakness in the slab, and then carefully break the slab along this line. The main problem with using paving slabs is establishing a proper gradient so that water drains off. In addition, once the slabs are set, you will need to fill the gaps between them with mortar in order to leave a smooth surface which you can clean easily.

A few budgerigar keepers prefer to lay a gravel base in the outside flight of their aviary. This will need to be 12.5cm(5in) deep, as it acts rather like the filter bed of an aquarium; the droppings and other debris are washed down through the gravel, out of reach of the budgerigars. This system works well in the part of the flight which is fully open to the elements, but under cover, droppings and, in the moulting season, feathers tend to accumulate beneath the perches and can be very difficult to remove. If you do decide to use gravel, set paving slabs in the most heavily used areas, so that the dirt can be scraped off more easily. Gravel is really only suitable as a floor covering in an aviary housing just a few budgerigars.

A permanent concrete base is generally the best option for the aviary floor. If you move at a later date and take the aviary with you, the new owners of your home will be able to use a concrete base as a site for a greenhouse or a patio area, should they not wish to keep birds of any kind. Whatever type of floor you decide to install in the flight, you will need to be able to keep it clean. Use a shovel to remove droppings under the perches and then hose the floor to ensure that it is thoroughly clean. During wet weather, unsightly algal growth may appear on the floor of the flight and you will need to scrub the concrete or paving slabs to remove such deposits.

The flight
Make the aviary in sectional form so that you can dismantle the structure without difficulty if you move house at a later date. Have a clear plan of the structure of the flight before you start. Wire mesh is usually sold in rolls approximately 90cm(3ft) wide and you can save yourself unnecessary work, and avoid wastage of materials, by constructing the flight around this dimension, for example 270cm(9ft) long, 180cm(6ft) high and 90cm(3ft) wide.

Sketch out the various components of the flight so that you can prepare a clear list of the lengths of timber you will need. You should be able to purchase these cut to size from a wood merchant. You will need to treat the timber with a safe non-toxic preservative. Various preparations are available that can be applied to untreated timber with a brush, but this can be a time-consuming task for even a small flight, especially as you will probably need to apply several coats. Lay the lengths of timber on a pair of trestles, with old newspaper beneath to catch any spillage. Alternatively, you can buy lengths of timber which have already been treated, but check that the chemicals used are not toxic, as budgerigars will often gnaw at the timber of the aviary.

When you are planning the flight unit, remember to allow for jointing the lengths of timber together. This serves to strengthen the overall structure and helps to prevent any buckling of the wood, which can itself weaken the aviary. Thicker timber, 5cm(2in) square, is recommended for outside use.

You will need a clear area of ground, with a readily accessible power supply, to handle the long timbers and make up the frames. Take great care when using electrical equipment out of doors, especially if the weather has been wet. Weatherproof the timbers and leave the wood to dry before assembling the individual frames. Paint cut ends with a suitable preservative, so that the whole frame will be protected from the elements. Screws are most suitable for fixing the component parts of the panels together,

Above: *Choose a sheltered spot for the aviary, away from trees, and which, if possible, will allow you to see the birds from indoors.*

although you can use nails of the appropriate length. Ensure that they are driven straight through the wood and do not split the sides.

The next task will be to cover the frames with mesh. Use 1.25cm(0.5in) square mesh rather than 2.5x1.25cm(1x0.5in), as used for the flight cage. Although more expensive, this will be more effective in excluding mice from the aviary, as the gaps in the mesh are much smaller. Buy a 30m(96ft) roll rather than 6m(20ft) lengths, which are relatively costly.

Lay the flight panel on a flat surface, and attach the mesh to the side which will ultimately form the inner surface of the flight. As with the flight cage, it is important to keep the mesh both straight and taut on the frames. Someone else's assistance at this stage can be very helpful. Once the mesh is fixed in place, insert extra netting staples around the sides to ensure that there are no areas of weakness. Over a period of time, the netting staples can pull out of the woodwork around the roof, which may be exposed to the weight of snow, and even cats (see *Keeping cats at bay*, page 34).

Having constructed the flight panels around the dimensions of the mesh, you should have no loose cut ends on the sides of the vertical sections of the framework. Trim back the top and bottom as far as possible, and cover with battening. You will probably need to replace this at intervals, as the budgerigars will gnaw at it.

The flight should not be left totally exposed to the elements. Translucent corrugated plastic sheeting fixed across the top section of mesh and extending at least 90cm(36in) from the shelter will protect the birds from wind and rain and ensure that water does not pour into the flight. Fix guttering at the edges as an additional precaution. Extend this plastic sheeting for a similar distance along the sides of the flight closest to the shelter, providing extra protection here. Special fitments can be used to anchor the sheeting firmly in place onto the aviary structure.

The shelter
The design of the shelter tends to be more variable than that of the flight unit. The cheapest option is a box-like structure incorporated at the rear of the flight, in which the birds can roost. This is sometimes described as a raised shelter. Access, in this instance, is usually

via the flight, with a small door at the front of the shelter giving access to the interior, where the budgerigars' food is located. Depending on the size of the flight, the shelter may occupy either the whole, or part of one end. It may even be supported on legs outside the flight, forming part of the exterior of the aviary. This design tends to be less secure, however, and if the birds manage to gnaw a hole in the wooden floor, they may escape from their quarters.

A full-length shelter attached to the flight will be more versatile than a raised house. Convert a small shed for this purpose, or construct a shelter on similar lines to those of the flight. In this instance, however, the roof will need to be sloped, and you will need to alter the dimensions of the framework accordingly. The highest point of the shelter should be at the junction with the flight; this will ensure that rainwater runs off away from the flight. Fix guttering to channel water to a soakaway or garden water butt.

Clad the sides of the shelter either in marine plywood or tongued-and-grooved timber, which looks more attractive, especially once it has been stained with a preservative. Both are efficient draught excluders. Cover the part of the shelter which connects directly with the flight with plywood though, as tongued-and-grooved boarding presents an irresistible challenge to gnawing budgerigars. Similarly, the roof of the shelter is best made of thick plywood, and should extend out over the sides of the shelter to enable rainwater to run off.

It is important to ensure that the inside of the shelter remains dry, so fill any obvious gaps with aquarium silicone sealant before applying a double layer of roofing felt on top. This should extend a short distance down the sides of the shelter, to minimize the risk of water leaking under the roof. Attach the felt with clout nails, ensuring that it is kept taut as you fix it in place. You can paint the felt

white to reflect the sun's rays and this should reduce the likelihood of it splitting prematurely. As an extra precaution, use broad battening to hold it in place in windy areas.

The aviary

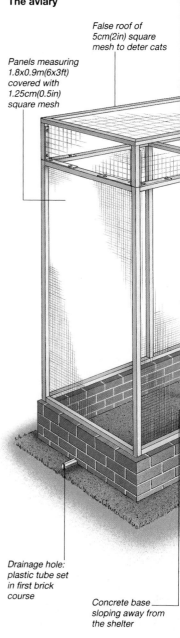

False roof of 5cm(2in) square mesh to deter cats

Panels measuring 1.8x0.9m(6x3ft) covered with 1.25cm(0.5in) square mesh

Drainage hole: plastic tube set in first brick course

Concrete base sloping away from the shelter

It is important that the aviary shelter is well lit, so that the budgerigars will be encouraged to roost inside. Set two windows, one in the side and one at the rear. You can buy double-glazed units quite cheaply, and simply slot them in as required. If possible, the windows should open; this will improve the ventilation in the shelter during the

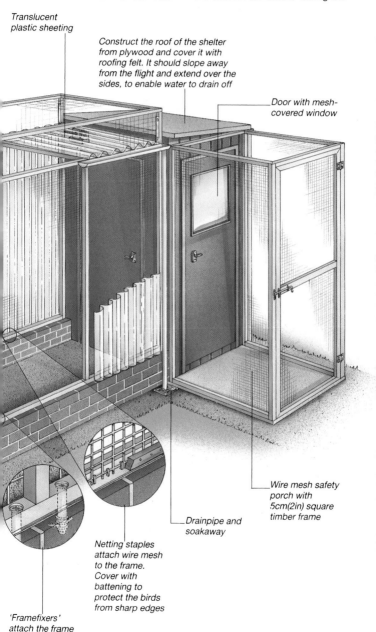

Translucent plastic sheeting

Construct the roof of the shelter from plywood and cover it with roofing felt. It should slope away from the flight and extend over the sides, to enable water to drain off

Door with mesh-covered window

'Framefixers' attach the frame to the brickwork

Netting staples attach wire mesh to the frame. Cover with battening to protect the birds from sharp edges

Drainpipe and soakaway

Wire mesh safety porch with 5cm(2in) square timber frame

The entrance to the shelter

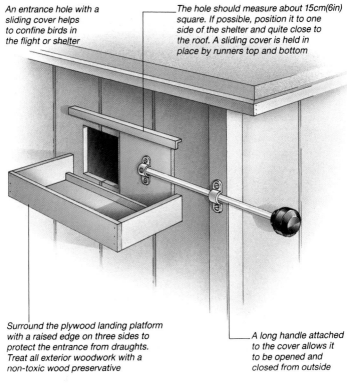

An entrance hole with a sliding cover helps to confine birds in the flight or shelter

The hole should measure about 15cm(6in) square. If possible, position it to one side of the shelter and quite close to the roof. A sliding cover is held in place by runners top and bottom

Surround the plywood landing platform with a raised edge on three sides to protect the entrance from draughts. Treat all exterior woodwork with a non-toxic wood preservative

A long handle attached to the cover allows it to be opened and closed from outside

summer and is particularly important for budgerigars nesting in the shelter during the breeding period. In any event, cover the windows on their inner surfaces with aviary mesh; otherwise, the birds may injure themselves as they attempt to fly through the opening, unaware that their path is blocked by a sheet of glass. It is a good idea to cover the remainder of the inside of the shelter with mesh, to prevent the budgerigars attacking the wooden framework with their beaks.

Obviously, you will need to have a door between the shelter and the flight to give you access to the latter. This should open into the flight. The budgerigars will also need to be able to move back and forth between the shelter and the flight. Cut a hole approximately 15cm(6in) square and 1.5m(5ft) off the ground. This can be

incorporated into the door, if necessary, but a separate exit for the birds is usually preferable. Make a landing platform, about 15cm(6in) across, on the shelter side, and edge it with thin plywood 'sides' extending to a height of 10cm(4in) above the base of the platform. This will prevent the wind blowing directly into the shelter.

It is useful to be able to close off this hole to confine the birds in either the shelter or the flight. If the entry hole is cut to one side of the shelter, you will be able to fit runners above and below the hole and set a cover into position that slides across the entrance. A wire loop will enable you to pull the cover back and forth as required. Line the floor of the shelter with sheets of old newspaper, which you will need to change once or twice a week. Avoid using coloured sheets, as hens in breeding condition will often resort to chewing the floor covering, and the inks on the paper could be harmful if swallowed.

The safety porch

You will need to have a safety porch to ensure that there is no risk of any of the birds escaping when you enter the aviary. Ideally this should adjoin the shelter as this is where the birds will be fed. It should not be necessary to walk through the flight each day to feed the birds – constant activity may disturb them and could cause them to desert their nests in the breeding season. If you decide on a small shelter, supported on legs outside the flight, you will need to incorporate a safety porch into the design of the flight. Some aviaries have two safety porches, one into the shelter and another into the flight, but this will inevitably add to the cost of constructing the aviary, and take up more space.

A safety porch adjoining the shelter need not be an elaborate affair; a useful size is 90cm(3ft) square and 1.8m(6ft) high, and a mesh porch will be the cheapest option. Hinge the door into the safety porch to open outwards, and the one adjoining the shelter so that it opens into the shelter. This will give you space to store cleaning equipment, such as brushes and buckets, inside, and you will be able to enter and close the door easily. Secure the door with a hook or bolt; it is a good idea to fix one on both sides of the door so that you can close it from the inside or the outside.

Assembling the aviary

Ideally, carry out as much of the 'component' construction work as possible – and ensure that the foundations have dried and are quite firm – before you attempt to erect the aviary on its base. Run strips of roofing felt on top of the foundations around the perimeter where the wooden frames will be positioned. These strips will act as a damp-proof course. Join the individual components of the

aviary together with bolts, held in place with both washers and nuts. The aviary should then be relatively easy to dismantle at a later date, if necessary. Mark and drill the holes for the bolts beforehand, so that instead of attempting to erect single frames, which are quite unstable, you will be able to manoeuvre supporting L-shaped sections into place on the base. You will need help at this stage, as these sections will be considerably heavier than single frames.

You can use bolts to fix the aviary in place on the foundations, but modern 'frame-fixers' are more effective. Whereas bolts are usually set with their heads embedded in the base, frame-fixers are passed down through the timber framework and felt lining into the bricks or blockwork. This will greatly simplify the construction process. Once the separate vertical sections of the aviary are in place, you can simply bolt on the roof section.

Perches in the aviary

The budgerigars will need perches in both the shelter and the flight. Again, natural branches are preferable (see page 19). After cutting them to the appropriate length and washing them as necessary, loop strands of wire tightly around the ends of the branches and fix them to the wooden framework of the aviary with netting staples. Do not site perches above one another or the lower perches will become soiled. The side shoots of a growing crown from a tree such as sycamore, planted in a large flowerpot, will provide additional perches for the budgerigars.

Dowelling perches, which can be held in place quite easily, are sometimes used in the shelter in preference to natural branches. Drill a hole of the appropriate size in a flat piece of plywood at least 12mm(0.5in) in thickness, fit the ends of the dowelling into these blocks and screw them to the sides of the shelter. Perches here should be higher than those in the

Above: *A rack system of perches can be constructed quite easily from dowelling and plywood, or bought from a specialist supplier.*

flight, to encourage the birds to roost in the shelter.

Rack perches are also popular and can be made quite easily. Fit a number of lengths of dowelling into two plywood holders, as described above, and position them so that they run on a slant, fitting within the shelter at an angle. Use a perch scraper with a blade to remove the droppings and keep the perches clean. These perches can be taken down and scrubbed clean as necessary.

Keeping cats at bay

While budgerigars will usually ignore cats in the vicinity of their aviary, and most cats similarly lose interest in the birds, certain individuals will prove more stubborn. You may need to deter the cat from sitting persistently on the aviary roof by modifying the design of the aviary. You can extend out strands of very thin mesh on supports around the roof of the aviary, to deter a cat from climbing up onto the structure. Another alternative is to construct a false roof which will also keep foxes off. You will need to construct an additional

wooden framework, approximately 30cm(1ft) high, and fix 22G mesh, about 5cm(2in) square, to all external sides. Use L-shaped brackets to secure this framework on the roof of the flight. Cats and foxes will not feel comfortable walking over this roof because of the wide gaps in the mesh and the lack of support beneath. This addition to the aviary need not look unsightly and could help to save the lives of your budgerigars. Although a cat on the aviary may not cause direct physical injury to the birds, recent research suggests that prolonged stress can be very harmful, particularly to exhibition budgerigars.

Vermin

You may also find that mice and even rats are attracted to the aviary, especially if there is seed on the floor of the flight. A hopper in the shelter will ensure that seed wastage is not a problem, and this should help to reduce the appeal of the aviary to vermin. Mice and rats are most likely to be seen after the summer, when food is becoming short. Since these rodents tend to be secretive, usually emerging to feed after dark, you may not actually see them, but their droppings, and the distinctive odour of their urine, will indicate their presence.

Mice may not harm the budgerigars directly, although they can disturb sitting hens, leading to losses of eggs and chicks. They do represent a definite health hazard though, since, by contaminating food and water in the aviary, they may transmit various diseases to the budgerigars. They will also be destructive, gnawing behind any lining material in the shelter or birdroom, for example.

The best means of defence against these rodents is to try to exclude them from the outset. Store seed in bins, rather than in paper sacks, use a fine mesh to prevent mice gaining access to the aviary (see page 29), and ensure that the base of the structure is solid. Within the confines of a birdroom, you can use an ultrasonic rodent deterrent as a further preventive measure. This piece of equipment operates at low cost off an electrical supply,

Below: *Storage bins like this one are ideal for keeping seed dry and will deter vermin. A scoop for removing the seed is also useful.*

emitting ultrasound waves which are disorientating for rodents and should drive them away. This device will not be harmful to the budgerigars themselves.

Unfortunately, it will not afford protection in the flight, since the ultrasound will rapidly dissipate here, and it may be a good idea to lay live traps instead. Look in the various birdkeeping journals for a design which does not permit the entry of the birds once set, in case a budgerigar becomes stuck in the entrance hole. Some designs of live trap can catch over ten mice during a single night, and provide an effective and safe means of eliminating these pests.

Poisons and killer traps are obviously hazardous in an environment where there is other livestock, but can be used as a last resort, provided that they are adequately screened out of reach of the birds themselves. For example, a trap of this kind can be set on the floor of the birdroom in an old breeding cage, with small holes cut in the bars to allow mice to enter easily, while excluding any budgerigars which may escape into this part of the aviary.

Rats may not be as numerous as mice, but they will often kill birds if they have an opportunity to do so. Look for burrowing activity around the aviary, which is often one of the first indicators of the presence of rats. Although you can set traps for rats, it is probably best to seek the advice of a professional pest control firm. Other predatory mammals, such as mink, could be responsible for the disappearance of birds from the aviary, and you will need experienced help to eliminate them.

Aviary maintenance
Check the exterior of the aviary at intervals, not only to deter rodents, but also to ensure that the structure remains waterproof. The felt will ultimately leak. Special products for flat roofs can be painted over it to form a seal. When weatherproofing the aviary, avoid painting the interior unless

you remove the budgerigars beforehand, and do not allow them back until the woodwork has dried completely. Provided that you have built it carefully and maintain it well, your aviary should last you for many years.

The birdroom
While a basic aviary of this type will enable you to keep a few breeding pairs of budgerigars together, it can be rather limiting. The likelihood of breeding success may also be reduced with the birds nesting communally (see *Breeding*, pages 60-71). You may decide, therefore, to opt for the larger structure of a birdroom, rather than just a basic aviary. Various options are open to you: you can buy a birdroom, or convert a suitable shed, or, if it is large enough, divide the existing shelter and use part of it as a birdroom.

In the simplest design, the birdroom is attached to one end of the flight. Part of the birdroom is partitioned off internally, using a wire mesh framework, and becomes the shelter. An outer safety porch surrounds the entrance to the birdroom, thus ensuring that all the occupants are safe within, provided you close the outer door of the safety porch before entering the birdroom.

There may be a window located in the door, or else at the front of the birdroom, alongside the flight. There should also be a window in the shelter area (see page 31). Several breeding cages can be stacked on the floor at the back of the birdroom on a wooden or metal framework holding them securely in place. There may also be space for an inside flight here, which can be useful for housing young stock prior to releasing them into the aviary, or as temporary holding quarters for birds which are to be sold. Other areas of space in the birdroom can be used for seed storage, and for training exhibition birds. You may also find it useful to have a clear table, ideally positioned directly in front of the window.

Lighting the birdroom
It will be useful to have an electrical supply running to the birdroom, but seek professional advice, as the regulations

Inside the birdroom

Extractor fan

Exhibition cages

Entrance hole with landing platform

Window in shelter covered on the inside with mesh

Tubular heater

The shelter is partitioned off internally with a wire mesh framework

governing the external supply of electricity can vary from one country to another. Electric lighting will enable you to feed the budgerigars after dark when necessary, which may be unavoidable during short winter days. The birds themselves will also benefit from increased lighting at this time of year, since they will

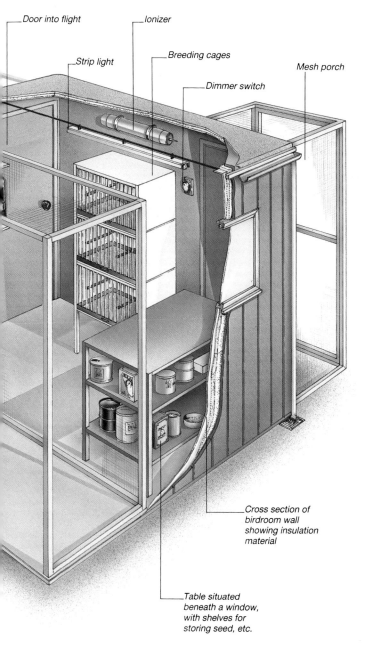

Door into flight

Ionizer

Strip light

Breeding cages

Dimmer switch

Mesh porch

Cross section of birdroom wall showing insulation material

Table situated beneath a window, with shelves for storing seed, etc.

have a longer period during which they can feed. Fluorescent strip lights, emitting a so-called 'natural' light, can also have positive health benefits for breeding budgerigars. The ultraviolet rays falling on the plumage of the birds stimulate the synthesis of Vitamin D3, which plays a vital part in controlling the body's stores of calcium. This is essential in the formation of egg shell, for example.

You can connect an electronic time switch, which will turn the lights on and off automatically, along with a dimmer, which will reduce the light intensity gradually. Thus, the budgerigars will not be plunged into sudden darkness, but will be able to return to their nests or roost before the lights go out. Various types of dimmer are available, the most sophisticated of which operate without being set to a time switch. When fixed close to a window, a photo-electric cell will trigger the lighting into operation once the level of illumination falls below a certain level. There are also dimmers which will work with fluorescent lights. These may have to be purchased from lighting shops or specialist birdkeeping suppliers.

Heating the birdroom

The use of heating for budgerigars is a controversial subject. Artificial heating can be useful, however, if you are breeding stock during the winter months in temperate climates, especially during sudden chilly spells. Cold conditions can lead to increased incidences of egg-binding (see page 64) in laying hens and, of course, young chicks are more vulnerable in cold weather. In conjunction with artificial lighting, therefore, a moderate degree of heat should help to ensure improved breeding results at this time of year.

Fan heaters are not suitable for use in birdrooms because the relatively high level of dust in the environment will interfere with their operation. Sealed electric tubular heaters, available in various sizes and wattages, are ideal; they are both durable and reliable and, unlike paraffin heaters, do not give off fumes which could be harmful to the birds. It is best to mount these heaters on the birdroom wall, rather than on the floor, to improve the circulation of air, and thus heat, through the building. You can obtain these heaters either from specialist avicultural suppliers or from garden centres, as they are also widely used in greenhouses. The wattages you will need for your birdroom will depend on various factors, including the size of the structure, the degree of insulation and the external temperature. The supplier will be able to advise you.

A thermostat connected to the heater unit will reduce the costs of heating the birdroom and ensure that the temperature does not fall below a minimum level. The simplest type of thermostat fits directly into the electrical socket, and the heater plug connects into the thermostat unit. Check the temperature range over which the thermostat will operate – this is usually between 0°C and 30°C(32-86°F) – and also that it is capable of operating all the heaters in the birdroom. As a general guide, you should set the thermostat to switch on the heating once the temperature falls to about 7°C(45°F) and to turn off the heaters when the temperature rises to 10°C(50°F). This way you will prevent the temperature in the birdroom falling excessively, even on a cold night, thus safeguarding both eggs and chicks.

Ventilation

The maintenance of a good air flow is an important, yet often forgotten, aspect to consider in planning a birdroom. Keeping a number of budgerigars together in a confined space will lead to the generation of a considerable amount of dust from their feathers, especially during the moulting period and, although this may not be harmful for the birds, it can lead to respiratory problems for their keepers. Typical symptoms of this

Above: *Birdrooms come in all shapes and sizes. This is a well-planned larger example, which incorporates running water and a sink. Note the first aid cabinet.*

allergic reaction – commonly known among pigeon fanciers as 'bird-fancier's lung' – are a tight-chested feeling and difficulty in breathing soon after entering the birdroom.

Obviously, windows will help to improve ventilation, but it is not always possible to leave them open, especially during bad weather. An extractor fan, as used in the home, will actively draw the air and accompanying dust from the birdroom but may also cool the air. Although some models can be rather noisy, the budgerigars will soon get used to this. You can connect the fan to a time switch so that it will operate on a regular basis, with a wire mesh cover to prevent a budgerigar which escapes into the birdroom being sucked into it.

Another means of combating dust in the birdroom is an ionizer. This piece of equipment has become very popular since its introduction to the avicultural market several years ago. The needle-like tip at the end of the ionizer emits a stream of high energy electrons which generate negative ions that pass through the air and collide with dust particles and other microscopic debris, including bacteria. Dust particles bombarded with these ions take on a negative charge and are drawn towards an earthed surface, such as the floor. You can then easily remove the accumulated dirt with a dampened piece of kitchen towelling. In addition to removing dust, an ionizer also helps to prevent the spread of airborne infections, by destroying bacteria.

If you do not have electricity in your birdroom, you will probably be able to run the ionizers successfully at very low cost off a car battery. Check that the model you purchase can be operated by this means. An ionizer is very straightforward to operate; simply position it at a high point in the birdroom and leave it switched on constantly. The difference in the atmosphere should become apparent within an hour or so. You will not need to screen the ionizer in any way, as it will not harm a budgerigar that escapes into the birdroom.

If a false wire door is fitted in the birdroom, you will be able to leave the outer birdroom door open on hot days, secure in the knowledge that the budgerigars are safely confined within, out of reach of cats and other predators.

Feeding budgerigars

The basic diet of budgerigars consists of the seed mixtures that you can obtain either from your local pet store or from a specialist seed supplier. To remain healthy, however, budgerigars also require minerals and greenfood.

Seed mixtures

Seed mixtures for budgerigars usually consist of two types of cereal seed; canary seed, which is brownish in colour and has pointed ends, and millet, which is rounded in appearance. Different types of millet may be apparent in a budgerigar seed mixture.

Canada and parts of North Africa, notably Morocco, are the major producers of canary seed, although crops from various other countries are occasionally available. It has been successfully grown in Europe – Spain used to be one of the main suppliers - and you should be able to cultivate this grass in the garden. Prepare the ground, choosing a sunny location as far as possible, and sow the seed in drills during the late summer. If space is limited, you can sprinkle a little canary seed towards the back of the flower border, since it is not an unattractive plant when growing. Thin the resulting seedlings as necessary before the winter, and cut the grass when the seedheads have turned brown during the following summer. There is no need for the grass to be ripe unless you want to store the seed, since budgerigars will delight in feeding on fresh green seedheads. You should only cut larger quantities once they are dry, and then hang the seedheads upside down in a shed. There is no need to worry about threshing the crop – the budgerigars will enjoy prizing the seeds from the seedheads.

Millet can be grown in a similar way, although it may prove less hardy. The different varieties likely to be encountered in seed mixtures include pearl white, which is a relatively large seed, and the smaller panicum and Japanese millets. Panicum can also be purchased in sprays and these are very popular with budgerigars.

Cheaper seed mixtures tend to contain a higher proportion of millet than canary seed. In terms of

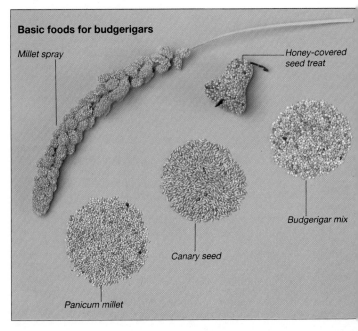

Basic foods for budgerigars

Millet spray

Honey-covered seed treat

Budgerigar mix

Canary seed

Panicum millet

their nutritional value, both are cereal seeds, and thus low in oil (fat) but with a relatively high carbohydrate content. Canary seed generally contains slightly more protein than millet, but samples do vary, depending on the local growing conditions and other factors, such as the relative use of artificial fertilizers. Some breeders prefer to feed a mixture of canary seed from various parts of the world in order to balance out nutritional shortcomings from any particular source.

Budgie seed mixes that are specially supplemented with vitamin and minerals are valuable, but avoid using extra supplements, which could then be harmful. Check advertisements in the birdkeeping journals for mail-order bird-seed suppliers, or buy seed directly from a pet store. Packeted brands sold here are subjected to strict quality control, whereas loose seed may, on occasions, be a source of problems. It might be contaminated by fodder mites (minute creatures seen moving among the seeds) or, worse still, by rodent droppings. Such problems are rare, but never purchase seed if you suspect that it could be of poor quality.

Always store seed in bins, rather than in sacks, to prevent it becoming damp and turning mouldy. This should also serve to deter rodents (see page 34).

Grit

Budgerigars need a regular supply of grit to assist them in the digestion of their food. They will dehusk seeds with their beaks, but lack any means of effectively chewing the kernel. The seeds pass through the crop, which acts as a storage organ, into the gizzard, a muscular organ with a thick wall. The particles of grit serve to macerate the kernels here, breaking them down into smaller particles on which the digestive enzymes can function effectively.

Cuttlefish

Seed tends to be a poor source of both minerals and trace elements

Below: *Budgerigars are very easy to cater for, requiring seed mix, grit and a regular supply of greenfood.*

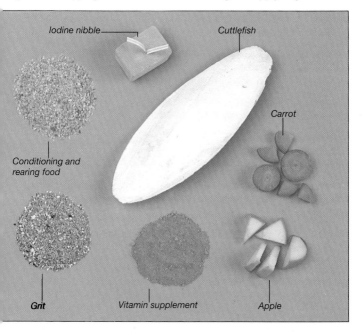

Iodine nibble

Cuttlefish

Carrot

Conditioning and rearing food

Grit

Vitamin supplement

Apple

Meadow grass

Spinach beet
leaves

Suitable greenfoods

Canary seed
grass

Chickweed

and other means of providing these will be necessary. Cuttlefish bone, sold by seed stockists, is a valuable source of calcium and, although it is especially important during the breeding period, budgerigars should have access to it throughout the year. You can obtain special clips which fit to the sides of the cage or aviary mesh to hold the bone in place without bending the mesh. It may be better to break the bone into small pieces to prevent it becoming soiled, which will happen if the budgerigar decides to use it as a perch.

Cuttlefishes, which are marine molluscs related to squids and octopuses, control their buoyancy by pumping water in and out of the multichambered 'bone'. If you live close to the beach, you may find these white bones washed up on the seashore, especially after storms. Only take clean bones home with you, avoiding any which are clearly contaminated with tar. Soak them in a bowl of fresh water, changing this at least once a day. After a week or so, dry the bones, either naturally out of doors or in an oven, and store.

Above: *It is easy to grow a variety of greenfood, which provides birds with a valuable source of vitamins.*

Greenfood
In addition to their basic seed diet, budgerigars will also benefit from a supply of greenfood on a regular basis. Even if you do not have access to a garden, you can still provide a fresh, uncontaminated supply for your pet. Simply fill a clean empty margarine tub with soil and sprinkle some budgerigar seed on top. Cover this with a thin layer of earth, place it in a warm spot, and keep it watered. The seeds will soon start to sprout and, once they have grown sufficiently – to several inches in height – you can cut off small amounts each day for your budgerigars.

You should be able to find a variety of greenfoods out of doors, but avoid sites where potentially harmful chemicals may have been used, such as roadside verges. Here, lead from engine exhausts may also have collected in the vegetation. The availability of greenfood is influenced to some extent by the season. Chickweed

(*Stellaria media*) is widely used by budgerigar keepers, and tends to be most prolific in the late spring and early autumn, although it is not difficult to maintain a supply in a shaded part of the garden, especially if it is kept well watered in dry weather. Towards the end of the summer you can collect seeding grasses, such as Meadow Grass (*Poa annua*).

Cultivated greenfoods can also be offered to budgerigars. You can grow spinach beet easily from seed and, even during the winter, it can be harvested for the birds. Allow it to warm up, however, if the temperature is below freezing. Various strains of spinach beet (*Beta vulgaris*) are available; choose one which contains low levels of oxalic acid, as this chemical can interfere with the absorption of calcium, an important mineral, particularly for breeding stock. Although budgerigars will often gnaw at the thicker stalks of spinach, chop up large leaves to prevent them becoming soiled with droppings. Lettuce is not a popular choice with most breeders, since it is said

Below: *Open food pots are useful, especially for feeding perishable items, such as soaked seed. Wash such containers between feeds.*

to lead to scouring (loose droppings), and although freshly cut lettuce, fed in moderation, will do no harm, it has little nutritional value compared with other vegetables. It is best to wash all greenstuff before feeding, as it may have been contaminated by a variety of wild creatures.

As winter proceeds, and greenfood is in short supply, you can offer your budgerigars washed, scraped carrots, either cut into pieces or grated. These are a valuable source of Vitamin A. Not all birds take carrot readily, and you may need to persevere to encourage a budgerigar to sample it. Avoid feeding carrot to exhibition budgerigars before showing them, however, as the juice may stain the facial feathering. Alternatively, you can offer a dessert apple, again cut into small pieces. By offering a wide variety of items to young birds, you should find that they eat such foods readily in later life.

Food supplements
All these fresh foods, when damp, also provide a convenient means of supplying the budgerigars with a nutritional supplement. Since most supplements are in powdered form, they will readily stick to damp food; sprinkled into a seed

pot, the powder will fall to the bottom and remain uneaten. Various powdered brands are available; select one that contains not only vitamins, minerals and trace elements, but also the essential amino-acids, which are the individual constituents of protein. Seed tends to be low in certain members of this group and so supplements are valuable.

Studies have shown that budgerigars require a relatively high amount of iodine. This is used by the thyroid glands, located in the neck region on either side of the windpipe, to produce hormones that influence various body processes, including moulting. A shortage of dietary iodine is likely to lead to the condition known as goitre, which results in an enlargement of the thyroid glands, possibly to as much as ten times their normal length of about 2mm(0.1in). This in turn causes pressure on the windpipe, and an affected bird may breathe noisily, because of the partial obstruction here. In aviary surroundings, you will probably be able to hear a bird suffering from this complaint when the birds are roosting and there is little background noise. Most supplements now contain iodine, but it is also worth giving budgerigars an iodine nibble, which you can fit into the bars of a cage or the aviary mesh.

Dietary extras
Various treats for budgerigars are widely available. These include seed rings, which fit around the perch, and feeding sticks, which attach to the side of the cage. But beware if these contain a colouring agent, as this may in turn affect the colour of the budgerigar's droppings.

For newly acquired birds, the use of a probiotic is recommended. This contains beneficial bacteria, which help to protect the gut from harmful micro-organisms. Electrolyte products are also useful after a journey or a show, when the bird may not have been drinking properly. They help to counter the effects of dehydration.

Food containers
There are a variety of bird feeding containers on the market, and many are suitable for use with budgerigars. Cages usually come equipped with two food pots, one at each end. You can fill these with seed and grit respectively, but take care to arrange the perches so that they do not directly overhang the containers, or droppings may contaminate the food. If the pot has a covered hood, start by sprinkling a little seed on the floor of the cage around the base of the feeding container to encourage young (and probably reluctant) budgerigars to place their heads under the hood to feed. Fixing a millet spray on the side of the cage close to a perch will also encourage a youngster to start feeding in new surroundings.

Metal seed hoppers are frequently used in aviaries as they are indestructible and keep the contents free from the birds' droppings. An enclosed tray, included in most designs, collects the seed husks and prevents them littering the floor of the shelter. Hoppers of this type are sold on the basis of their seed capacity and the number of feeding holes for the budgerigars. A large capacity hopper will save time, and you can be certain that the budgerigars have sufficient seed to last them several days. This can be particularly useful at holiday times, when someone else will have to look after them. Do not be tempted just to leave the birds over a weekend though, even if they have plenty of seed and water available, since one may fall sick or be injured. They need to be checked once, and preferably twice, a day.

Special plastic bases which fit around the base of upturned jam jars are often used in box-type cages, but are not suitable for most ordinary cages, since the doors are too small to allow the seed reservoir to be placed inside. Plastic tubular containers, some of which can be refilled from outside the cage, provide a more versatile means of feeding budgerigars in cages. It is important, however, especially with narrow-spouted feeders of this type, to ensure that the flow of seed is not impeded.

These containers can also be used for water, but you will need to change the water daily and thoroughly wash the vessels each week. If you have added a tonic or medication to the water you will need to wash the container before refilling it. Tubular drinkers can be difficult to clean; use a bottle-brush of the appropriate size, especially for the spout. Drinkers of this type, like feeders, are supplied with special clips which attach to the sides of the cage or aviary. In the aviary, it is important to position tubular drinkers out of the direct rays of the sun, as far as possible, otherwise they will

become rapidly contaminated with greenish algal growth. It is worth having one or two spare drinkers available so they can be rotated for cleaning purposes and so that a replacement is on hand if needed.

Never fill drinkers to the top during cold weather or the container may split as the water freezes. For the same reason, you should avoid pouring boiling water over the plastic to melt the ice. Float the drinker in warm water and within a few moments the ice plug will be dislodged from the interior of the drinker, which you can then refill. When a large number of budgerigars are being kept in cages, as in a birdroom during the breeding period, an automatic drinking system may be worth considering. Several systems of this type are available.

A plastic seed tray is ideal to prevent greenstuff being pulled onto the floor. Greenfood racks, which are sold for use in both cages and aviaries, are ineffective; the budgerigars simply pull the leaves out of the rack.

Below: *A selection of the utensils used to provide food and water. Larger hoppers are available for aviaries to minimize wastage.*

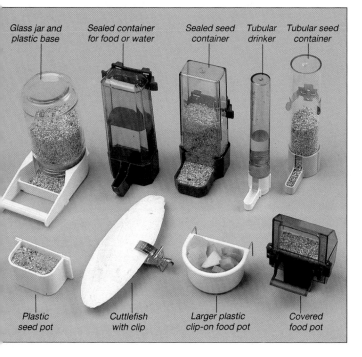

Glass jar and plastic base

Sealed container for food or water

Sealed seed container

Tubular drinker

Tubular seed container

Plastic seed pot

Cuttlefish with clip

Larger plastic clip-on food pot

Covered food pot

Caring for your budgerigar

Keep a close watch on a newly acquired young budgerigar for the first few days to check that it settles in without problems. If the bird is eating well there is unlikely to be any cause for concern. Most recently fledged budgerigars are naturally tame, although they may be rather nervous at first.

Taming your budgerigar
Obviously, the more time that you spend with a young budgerigar the more tame it is likely to become. Encourage it to perch on your hand at every opportunity, for example by holding a millet spray just out of the budgerigar's reach. Placing your finger parallel with the perch where the budgerigar is sitting will encourage the bird to step onto your hand, especially if you slowly move your finger upwards to effectively dislodge its grip on the perch. Take care not to frighten the budgerigar by sudden movements, however, as this will retard the taming process.

Once the budgerigar is perching readily on your finger, you can persuade it to leave the cage. Do not be surprised if, as you

withdraw your finger with the bird, it steps off at the last minute. You may find it easier to catch the bird in the cage and then place it on your finger again once you are sitting in the room. However, if your budgerigar is allowed to fly around the room, you may have difficulty in catching it.

A number of potential dangers exist in a room, ranging from windows and cats to uncovered fish tanks and poisonous plants. Before opening the cage door, always take care to ensure that the windows in the room are closed and, preferably, covered with net curtains. There will then be no risk of a budgerigar which escapes from your hand flying directly at the glass, which could prove fatal. Cats are another potential hazard, and should be excluded from the room during training sessions, if only because they may upset the bird. You should also remove any ornaments which could be knocked over.

Below: *Finger taming is quite easy if you start with a young budgerigar about six weeks old.*

Wing clipping

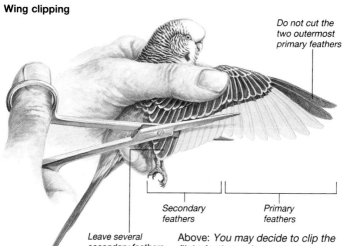

Do not cut the two outermost primary feathers

Secondary feathers

Primary feathers

Leave several secondary feathers close to body intact

Above: *You may decide to clip the flight feathers of one wing to prevent your budgerigar injuring itself when flying in the room. These cut feathers will be moulted.*

You may have difficulty in getting the budgerigar back into the cage at first. It is a good idea to draw the curtains, so that the room is as dark as possible; this should ensure that the budgerigar remains in one place, allowing you to reach it easily. Take care to free its claws carefully before lifting it back to the cage. Given time, you should be able to train the budgerigar to fly around the room and then return to the cage of its own accord, but on the first few occasions you will almost certainly have to return it to the cage yourself. Place a landing platform, available from pet stores, on the outer side of the cage door, to encourage the bird to fly in.

If you have a large flight cage, there is no real need to let the bird out into the room. Nevertheless, you cannot fully enjoy your pet if it is not allowed to join you in the room, so provided you take the necessary precautions, you can allow the budgerigar to fly around while you are present.

Wing clipping
You may decide to clip the feathers of one wing, so as to handicap your pet's flight. This will help to protect the budgerigar from injury when flying around the room, and it will also make it easier for you to catch it. The procedure, if carried out properly, is both quick and painless, but should you be in doubt, obtain expert advice beforehand. Open the wing and, leaving the two outermost primary feathers and several of the secondary flight feathers closest to the body intact, cut across the remaining feathers with a sharp pair of scissors. It will be easier if you have someone to hold the budgerigar for you. Never cut right down to the base of the shaft, as this may cause severe bleeding if the feather is relatively new and still receiving a blood supply. Wing clipping, carried out in this way, is not disfiguring, and provides a temporary means of restricting your budgerigar's flight skills. The cut feathers will be shed and replaced at the next full moult, and you can then repeat the procedure if necessary.

Toys
A variety of toys are available for pet budgerigars, but is is important not to clutter the cage with them, which will prevent the bird from

moving around easily. Budgerigars often prefer the least elaborate toys, which may also prove the safest. Avoid designs which could be easily destroyed, or are held together with sharp projections which, if exposed, could injure your bird. There is also a risk that a playful budgerigar could get caught up on certain toys. For example, it is not unknown for slim budgerigars to become lodged between the rungs of a toy ladder while trying to squeeze through them. You will also need to consider carefully the means of attaching toys to the cage. Never use string or threads, which the budgerigar may eat, with potentially fatal consequences.

Some pet owners will not use a mirror in their bird's cage, for fear that seeing its reflection will discourage the budgerigar from talking. There appears to be no truth in this belief, but your budgerigar may attempt to feed its reflection, and even regurgitate seed. If this develops into a regular habit, you should remove the mirror for several weeks. This behaviour is probably linked with a desire to breed, and cock birds tend to be worse in this regard than hens. The phase should pass, but occasionally the problem

Above: *Various kinds of toys appeal to budgerigars. Choose simple ones that will not hurt your pet and that you can clean easily.*

becomes so severe that the bird, continually regurgitating seed, starts to lose weight. Change the budgerigar's environment by moving it to another part of the house, or even by transferring it to a new cage. This will often prove effective therapy. Do not confuse this behaviour with the ailment known as 'sour crop' (see page 54), where the crop itself becomes distended and the budgerigar's appetite wanes.

A final point to consider when choosing toys is that they should be easy to clean. Avoid toys such as the open-weave plastic balls, with a bell at the centre, for this reason. As a plaything of this type, an ordinary table-tennis ball is preferable, since you can easily remove droppings from it with a damp piece of paper towel.

Bathing
Another useful piece of equipment for the cage is a plastic bird bath. This will enable your budgerigar to bathe without splashing water onto surrounding furniture. A typical design fits over the cage door, and

a modified version is available in the form of a small shower, which operates when the budgerigar steps onto the edge of the unit. Not all budgerigars are keen to bathe of their own accord, however, so you may prefer to spray your bird once or twice a week, to keep its plumage in top condition. A clean plastic plant sprayer is ideal for this purpose. Fill it with tepid water and then, having removed food and grit pots, spray the budgerigar, directing the jet of water so that droplets fall onto the bird from above. Although your bird may appear nervous at first, it will soon come to appreciate a regular bath.

Talking skills
The vocal repertoire of the budgerigar can exceed that of most parrots. Indeed, one of the most famous talking budgerigars ever known, named 'Sparkie Williams', learned no less than eight complete nursery rhymes, (taught in individual lines), as well as nearly 360 phrases, and his complete vocabulary extended to over 550 words. Shortly before his death in 1962, Sparkie became a

recording star, selling 20,000 copies of his record, and featuring in several radio programmes.
Although Sparkie's skills were exceptional, it is not difficult to teach a budgerigar to talk successfully. Start by choosing a simple phrase – linking perhaps 'Hello' with your bird's name – and repeat this every time you enter the room or approach the cage. Within a few weeks, your budgerigar should be able to repeat this. You can then expand its repertoire, for example, by saying 'Good night' when you cover the cage at night. (It is best to restrict the effective daylength for your budgerigar to about 12 hours in this way. Choose a plastic cover rather than a material one as your budgerigar's claws could become caught up in the threads.)
As the bird starts to learn to mimic words and sounds, you can continue expanding its vocabulary, but do not omit to run through previously taught phrases, otherwise these may be forgotten. The teaching process can be reinforced by using cassette tapes. It is also possible to buy special records and pre-recorded tapes to encourage your bird to talk, but as the voice will be strange to the bird, they may prove less effective.
Your budgerigar's talking skills can help to reunite you if the bird

Below: *You will find it more effective to teach a budgie to talk yourself, rather than rely on special cassette tapes or records.*

escapes. Try, therefore, to teach it either the address of your house, or a telephone number, so that anyone finding the budgerigar will, hopefully, be able to return it to you. Every year, a number of pet budgerigars escape, especially during the summer when windows are left open. Your local radio station or newspaper may prove a useful means of recovering your pet if it has escaped, as they often have 'lost and found' spots. Budgerigars may survive for several days, particularly when they have access to bird seed provided for wild birds, but generally they are unable to live for long under these conditions – their bright coloration makes them a clear target for cats.

Old age

The lifespan of budgerigars varies quite widely – pet birds often live for seven or eight years but exhibition budgerigars usually have a shorter lifespan. Occasionally, these parakeets survive well into their teens, and even twenties. In old age, budgerigars often become less active, but there are normally few obvious signs of ageing.

The moulting period becomes extended in old budgerigars. This should not be confused with so-called 'soft-moult', which often occurs in budgerigars kept indoors, when they shed odd feathers on a regular basis, as well as moulting more intensively over a few weeks. Older budgerigars typically retain a large number of 'spikes' just above the cere when moulting. These are new feathers, still wrapped in their protective sheaths, which normally unravel quickly in younger birds. The budgerigar's thyroid glands may slow down with age and you can supply a special hormonal supplement (available at low cost from your veterinarian) to help at this time of year.

Budgerigars are also more prone to tumours of various types in old age. See pages 54-5 of *Basic health care* for further details of symptoms and treatment.

Catching aviary budgerigars

There will be times when you need to catch a budgerigar from the aviary and this may prove difficult at first. Start by shutting the birds in one part of the aviary and then take the perches down to give you more space. You will probably find it easier to catch the birds with your hands rather than use a net, especially in a relatively confined space. Try to restrain the budgerigar on the aviary mesh, by cupping your hands around it.

If you prefer to use a net for catching your budgerigars, be sure to obtain one that has thick padding around the rim to minimize the risk of injury should you accidentally miss the bird. A deep net is also recommended to prevent the budgerigar flying out again once caught. You can obtain catching nets of this type from specialist suppliers. Try to trap the budgerigar when it is on the aviary mesh. Once it is in the net, place your hand over the top, holding the rim, and then reach inside to restrain the bird. Hen birds, in particular, may give you a painful bite, so try to locate the head of the bird first. You may want to wear a thin pair of gloves when you are handling your budgerigars, to help give you confidence until you are familiar with restraining them. Remember, however, that gloves will reduce your sensitivity, so take extra care not to injure the birds. Never attempt to lift a budgerigar straight out of the net because its claws will almost certainly be gripping the material. Gently free each claw in turn before releasing the net and transferring the bird to a box. Although you can use a cage for this purpose, this is not recommended if you hope to show the bird in the near future, as the budgerigar may damage its plumage on the bars. If you are taking the budgerigar out of the aviary, be sure to check that the container is securely closed so that the bird cannot escape.

Above: *You can use a net to catch budgerigars in aviary surroundings. Be sure that the rim is well padded to minimize the risk of injuries.*

Handling budgerigars
Correct handling of budgerigars is important to protect the bird and to prevent it biting you! Shift the bird's head carefully, so that it lies between the first and second fingers of your left hand, if you are right-handed, keeping the budgerigar's back and wings restrained in the palm of your hand. Never grip the bird's neck tightly with your fingers as this is likely to interfere with its breathing. Use your thumb and other fingers to gently restrain the front of the budgerigar's body, effectively encircling it. When held in this way, the bird will not be able to bite, yet most of the body is easily accessible, including the wings, which you can open in turn as required, with your other hand.

Correct

Incorrect

Basic health care

Few birds are easier to keep than budgerigars, but inevitably, individuals do fall ill from time to time. In many cases, provided that the symptoms are recognized early, there is no reason why the affected budgerigar should not be treated successfully and make a full recovery.

It is not usually difficult to spot a sick budgerigar – it will be less active than its companions, often remaining on the perch as you approach, while the other birds fly away. The plumage may be fluffed up and lose its sleek appearance, while other more specific signs, such as staining around the vent, may also be evident. Sick budgerigars often attempt to carry on feeding, and may even spend more time than usual picking at the seed, but closer examination usually reveals that the bird has simply been dehusking the kernels. (Canary seeds are darker when dehusked.) In such circumstances, it is best to catch the budgerigar and feel for signs of weight loss around the breastbone (see *Choosing a budgerigar*, page 14).

General care of sick budgerigars
You will need to isolate a sick budgerigar and keep it warm in order to assist its recovery. Maintain a temperature of around 32°C(90°F) using an infrared lamp, obtainable from specialist avicultural suppliers. Choose a model designed specifically for use with livestock which will not shatter if it is splashed and supplies only heat and no light. You should be able to buy a complete kit, including a thermostat, infrared bulb, the necessary cable and a holder. Some designs fit easily onto the front of a breeding cage, and it is well worth having a unit of this type available for use as a hospital cage in an emergency. Wash this cage thoroughly after use with a solution of disinfectant, so that it will be ready again when required.

Tempt the budgerigar's appetite with a millet spray, positioned within easy reach of the bird.

Above: *Keeping a sick budgerigar warm in a hospital cage may be vital to its recovery. Do not hesitate to seek veterinary advice.*

Water, too, should be readily available. If you are using a soluble powder treatment, such as an antibiotic, provide just one drinker containing the medication. Given a choice of medicated and non-medicated drinkers, the budgerigar is more likely to drink the untreated water rather than the antibiotic solution, which tends to have a bitter taste, and this would clearly lessen the likelihood of recovery.

In most cases, you should see signs of improvement after three days of treatment. You can then gradually lower the temperature by means of the control on the infrared lamp. If, however, the budgerigar's condition appears to worsen, and it continues to perch for long periods directly in front of the lamp, you will need to raise the temperature again to lessen the bird's discomfort, and then slowly repeat the process of lowering the temperature to cool off the bird.

It is best not to hurry a sick bird's return to an aviary, and you should certainly not return it to an outside flight when the weather is bad. You may have to keep it in a stock cage until weather conditions improve.

First aid kit

You will find it useful to have various items available for routine health care or in case of an emergency. You will need a styptic pencil to control minor bleeding, which may occur following a torn claw, for example. Alternatively, keep a supply of powdered alum (potassium aluminium sulphate), which you can make into a solution to curb blood loss. It is also worthwhile having a tube of ophthalmic ointment available to deal with any minor eye inflammation. You will need to apply the ointment directly to the affected eye, several times a day, and it is best to hold the budgerigar for a few minutes afterwards, so that it does not wipe the ointment off on the perch. Ointment, although easy to apply, does tend to matt the plumage, however, and so for exhibition budgerigars, eye drops may be preferable. However, you may find a solution of this type harder to administer – if the budgerigar blinks, it will scatter the fluid. An eye dropper is useful for dispensing medicine directly into the mouth. A pair of bone clippers, stocked by larger pet stores and grooming parlours (where they are used to trim dogs' toe nails), will be a valuable acquisition to cut back overgrown claws or beaks.

Claw and beak trimming

You will probably need to clip the budgerigar's claws from time to time to enable it to perch comfortably. The beak, once trimmed, will tend to grow back faster, so avoid clipping it, if at all possible.

Do not use scissors for trimming claws or beaks, as they tend to tear the tissue rather than cutting straight through it. Carry out this task in a bright area, so that you can identify the blood supply, which, in the claws, appears as a narrow red line extending down each claw from the base of the toe. Clip a short distance away from the end of this to prevent bleeding. You may find it harder to locate the blood supply in the beak. Look for a dark, triangular area on the inner surface of the upper beak, and clip below the lower point. The lower beak is easier to trim when necessary; simply cut back the surplus growth in line with the remainder of this part of the mandible. If in doubt, seek your veterinarian's advice.

The problems dealt with below are those which most frequently afflict budgerigars. You should, in any case, approach your veterinarian if your budgerigar shows signs of sickness.

Below: *You can cut back overgrown claws quite easily using a sharp pair of clippers. Make sure that you have adequate light.*

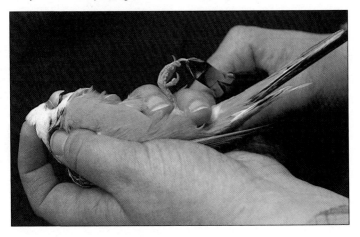

Enteritis

Studies suggest that budgerigars are perhaps most susceptible to digestive problems, which are frequently collectively described as 'enteritis'. Typical symptoms are lethargy and an alteration in colouring of the bird's droppings, which may become bright green and even be tinged with blood on occasions. In a healthy bird, the lining of the gut is protected by a beneficial population of bacteria, but a disturbance to these micro-organisms may enable other, harmful, bacteria to gain access. This is likely to trigger an infection. Your veterinarian may be able to arrange cultures from an affected budgerigar's droppings in order to establish the likely cause of infection, but this takes time. You should, therefore, administer an antibiotic medication before obtaining results of any such examination. Be sure to follow the instructions for usage very carefully. Overdosing will tend to worsen rather than improve the situation, because it may destroy more of the beneficial bacteria. Underdosing or ceasing treatment prematurely, however, often allows the harmful bacteria to continue replicating, and they may also become resistant to the treatment.

Although not all forms of enteritis are infectious, you would be wise to remove the affected budgerigar to a hospital cage (see page 52) and to clean the aviary thoroughly, especially food and water pots and perches, which may have been contaminated. The use of a probiotic (see page 44) will help the budgie's recovery.

Sour crop

This is a relatively common ailment, caused by the presence of a microscopic parasite in the crop called *Trichomonas*. This illness is also known as trichomoniasis. These parasites can be spread by adult birds feeding each other, while chicks often acquire the infection in the nest. Affected chicks may die quite rapidly.

Symptoms in older budgies include retching, which results in deposits of mucus being evident on the head. The crop at the base of the neck is likely to be distended with air, and contains little food. Empty the crop by gently massaging it up towards the throat, while holding the bird upside down. Medication added to the drinking water should soon resolve the problem, but it is often advisable to treat all the birds following an outbreak, in the hope of eliminating the infection entirely, otherwise it can become a persistent problem.

Other internal parasites are quite rare in budgerigars, compared with external mites (see *Choosing a budgerigar*, page 15), but they can occur on occasions. Roundworms, for example, can be diagnosed from a faecal sample, and are treated easily.

Tumours

Budgerigars are prone to tumours of various types. Watch for any swellings which appear on your bird's body, particularly as it gets

Below: *In some cases, you may need to administer medicine directly into a bird's crop. Your veterinarian can advise you.*

Above: *Note the very pale colour of this hen's cere. This can be a sign of chronic poor health, associated with a tumour.*

older. Lipomas, which consist of fatty tissue, are benign (non-cancerous) and may be removed by surgery, depending partly on their position. A common site is close to the breastbone, and here, especially, a lipoma will soon handicap the bird's flight, so that it cannot fly any distance. The development of lipomas may be linked, to some extent, to lack of exercise, since they are far less common in budgerigars housed in aviary surroundings.

More insidious in onset are internal tumours, which usually prove fatal. The reproductive organs are a common site; a tumour here will ultimately affect the cere coloration, turning this brownish in a cock bird, and pale, almost whitish, in hens. The kidneys may be similarly affected, and the bird will lose weight. Again, you should be able to detect such weight loss over the breastbone. The budgerigar will become progressively weaker, although it may appear to maintain its appetite. In the terminal stages, the bird will be unable to perch as the tumour will affect the spinal cord close to the kidneys. Obviously, by this stage, it will not

be fair to keep your bird suffering. Take the budgerigar to your veterinarian who will painlessly euthanase it, usually by injection.

There is a possibility that some tumours could be caused by viruses, so always disinfect and rinse the cage thoroughly should you subsequently decide to obtain another budgerigar.

Chlamydiosis

There are a few diseases which can be spread from budgerigars to people, of which the most notorious and well publicized is chlamydiosis (formerly known as psittacosis). This disease generally proves fatal for the birds.

The likelihood of people contracting chlamydiosis, which can also affect cats and a wide range of other animals and birds, is slight, but if you have sick budgerigars and you or any member of your family who could have been in contact with them develops symptoms of a bad bout of influenza or pneumonia, mention this possibility to your doctor.

Modern antibiotics have ensured that, provided the disease is diagnosed early, the chances of recovery for infected people are good. Certainly, on statistical grounds, there is no need to be put off keeping budgerigars through fear of contracting chlamydiosis. However, as a precaution, and as a means of monitoring the health of your flock, it is worthwhile having post mortem examinations carried out on budgerigars which die. Your vet will be able to advise you on having autopsies carried out.

It is also now possible to test living budgerigars for chlamydiosis, by means of a swab taken from the cloaca. This enables the health of new birds to be checked before they are released alongside existing stock, and should help to prevent the spread of this disease.

Always wash your hands thoroughly after handling a sick budgerigar, to avoid the risk of transmitting disease to other birds or contracting it yourself.

Exhibiting budgerigars

The earliest records trace competitive budgerigar exhibiting to the late 1870s, when the birds were exhibited either in classes alongside other parakeets or as pairs on their own. Exhibition budgerigars became less common for a period during the early years of the present century, and individual classes were then dropped from many show schedules. Nevertheless, after the First World War interest in the new colour varieties continued to grow and the exhibition side of the hobby received a considerable boost with the formation of the Budgerigar Club in 1925. A standard show cage for these parakeets was then devised and in February 1926 there were over one hundred entries at the first Budgerigar Club Show. Within ten years, this figure had risen tenfold. The name of the 'Budgerigar Club' was changed to the 'Budgerigar Society' in 1930, at the request of King George V, when he agreed to become patron.

Budgerigars are now shown, or 'benched', individually rather than as pairs, although there are team classes at larger shows. They are judged according to a scale of points, which differs somewhat in detail according to the variety concerned, although the ideal physical appearance of the budgerigar is a constant feature. The appearance of exhibition budgerigars differs significantly from that of aviary birds and in order to obtain an accurate impression of the qualities of winning stock, try to visit as many shows as possible. You will then be able to see the type (physical attributes) of the birds being selected by the judges. This will be of immense value when you start to set up your own stud.

Setting up a stud
Try to obtain your foundation stock from just a few sources. Many experienced breeders are keen to help beginners, and are well placed to advise on the pairings of budgerigars which they themselves have bred. Although you should try to pair up the birds with a view to compensating for the drawbacks in one partner with the strengths of the other, there is no guarantee that the chicks will follow this pattern. You may even find that the positive characteristics present in one individual are diluted in the offspring. Correct pairing of the birds is a crucial step towards subsequent show successes, so do not hurry this task. If you have joined the national Budgerigar Society, you may well be able to turn to a local, more experienced fellow member for advice. Continual and honest assessment is the only way to improve the quality of your emerging stud. Consider your first-year youngsters carefully once they have moulted out and dispose of those that show obvious weaknesses. Some of the adult birds may also be surplus to your requirements after the breeding season, depending on your stocking capacity.

Preparing for a show
There is more to budgerigar exhibiting than merely producing a bird which excels in type and colour. Preparation is a vital part of successful exhibiting, and the budgerigars must be trained for this purpose. They should be confident within the show cage – these are usually standard for exhibiting budgerigars – and such training can begin early in life. Handling chicks when you clean out the nestbox provides early contact, helping to familiarize them with human company, and you can continue to do this after weaning. It can be useful to house the young budgerigars individually in the show cage at this stage for short periods (not more than one hour a day) to familiarize them with these new surroundings.

Announcements of show dates and venues can be found in the various birdkeeping journals. If you are interested in entering an event, send a stamped self-addressed envelope to the show secretary for

Above: *Budgerigar shows are competitive events where the birds being exhibited are assessed according to set standards.*

a schedule, which will list the classes and other relevant information. Read and complete this carefully and return it well in advance of the closing date, to allow for postal delays. Don't forget to include your entry fees as well! This will be acknowledged, and you should also receive cage labels for the event.

Exhibitors evolve their own systems for managing their budgerigars before a show, and this depends to some extent on the birds themselves. Some budgerigars are natural exhibition birds; they are relatively tame and can usually be relied upon to perform well in front of the judge. Others will be more prone to skulking on the floor of the cage during judging! Catch the budgerigars and transfer them to individual stock cages several days before the show, being sure

to handle them carefully to avoid damage to their plumage. If their plumage is soiled you will need to wash the birds. Use baby shampoo, taking care to avoid the eyes. You may also need to trim the mask now to remove any additional spots. The ideal is considered to be two full circular spots on either side of the head, with an additional spot located at the bottom of the cheek patches. You can use tweezers to remove the excess feathering, or else carefully cut the plumage away with a small pair of scissors. A gentle spray with tepid water will help the rest of the feathering to look at its best.

The condition of the cage is also important. It must be fully intact, with no pieces missing, and in a general state of good repair. Regular painting may be necessary and cages should be washed out thoroughly after the show. Once completely dry, they can be stored in large plastic bags, tied at the end, until they are needed again.

You may want to use a special

Above: *Conditioning is a vital part of successful exhibiting. Spray the birds regularly to keep their plumage in good condition.*

show cage carrier to move the cages easily and cause minimum upset to the birds themselves. Try to reach the show relatively early, so that the budgerigars will be able to settle down before judging takes place and show themselves to best effect. Only show exhibition budgerigars when they are in top condition. Moulting individuals are best left at home, even though this means forfeiting the entry fee, which you will probably have had to pay in advance. Such birds are most unlikely to win and more prone to minor ailments in this state.

Feel at liberty to speak with the judge after the results have been announced. Alternatively, you may like to volunteer as a steward at a show so that you can gain a closer

view of the proceedings. In this way, you can learn the individual strengths and weaknesses of the birds being exhibited, which will assist you in the development of your own stud.

Development of the stud
If you have a budgerigar which is doing very well on the show bench, it is almost inevitable that sooner or later you will receive an offer from a fellow fancier wishing to purchase the bird. If you want to capitalize on your earlier hard work you should consider carefully

Right: *You may require expert help to trim the mask of an exhibition budgie prior to a show. The purpose is to create the symmetrical pattern shown on the far right by removing surplus feathering from the mask with a pair of tweezers. Not all varieties have a mask; the throat spots are not present in lutinos, for example.*

before accepting. The best studs have achieved the means of producing numbers of budgerigars that share not only physical similarities, but also close ancestral traits and genetic links. This is usually achieved by careful pairings of related birds. Line-breeding entails the mating of budgerigars sharing a common ancestry, whereas in-breeding is a refined form of line-breeding, which may entail pairing of son to mother, or daughter to father. Pairing budgerigars which are so closely related is not without its hazards, since although there is a likelihood that desirable characteristics will be enhanced, there is an equal risk that faults will be replicated. In-breeding is therefore only to be recommended with budgerigars of top quality, where the benefits should outweigh the potential drawbacks.

It is probably safest to evolve two distinct lines within your stud, so that if one encounters problems you can fall back on the other bloodline. Most exhibition breeders will specialize, selecting a group of colours which appeal to them.

At times, you will need to obtain new budgerigars for your stud. It is often easier to purchase cock birds of quality for 'out-crossing' – the introduction of unrelated stock,

usually excelling in a particular feature which may be lacking in your current stud. Good hens tend to attract a premium price.

Although you may be able to buy winning budgerigars (at a high price), you will not be able to guarantee your continuing success on the show bench unless you carefully develop this foundation stock to best effect. Careful record keeping plays a vital part in this process, and you should carefully log the pedigrees of each bird, either in a card index or on computer. You can then refer back easily when deciding on pairings for the next breeding season. Your constant aim should be to improve the overall quality of your stud.

Another factor to be considered is the type of plumage. Feather type can be divided into a soft yellow form and a much coarser buff variety. This is a physical feature, not connected with the bird's colour. Although buff birds may appear somewhat larger, since the plumage is not sleek, repeated pairing of buff to buff (termed 'double buffing') is detrimental because the plumage becomes excessively coarse, spoiling the bird's appearance. Crossing with budgerigars of a yellow feather type will ensure that a balance is maintained.

Breeding and rearing

Budgerigars are not usually difficult birds to breed as pairs normally nest readily. To ensure that breeding stock is fully mature, do not use birds under about 10 months old. Cocks tend to have a longer reproductive life than hens, and will sire chicks successfully when eight or nine years old. Most exhibition breeders tend to concentrate on breeding from budgerigars during their second and third years, and so you may be able to obtain older quality stock at a relatively low price.

Nestboxes

You can buy budgerigar nestboxes from many pet stores or from specialist suppliers advertising in birdkeeping magazines. Various designs are available; opt for one which enables you to check the interior easily, and which you can clean without difficulty. Nestboxes with hinged lids are not really suitable therefore. Breeders most commonly use a box which opens at one end, usually with an outer sliding plywood door with a piece of glass behind it. This will prevent eggs or chicks falling out when you slide the outer door vertically upwards in the runners. The interior of the nestbox is lined with a so-called 'concave'. This is a flat piece of wood, with a depression hollowed out, usually at one end. Here the hen will lay her eggs, and the concave will help to prevent them being scattered when she leaves the nestbox. Place this away from the entrance hole so that the birds are less likely to damage the eggs as they move in and out of the nestbox. Some breeders place this concave within a wooden box, the sides of which

Basic nestbox

Entrance hole

Simple plywood box

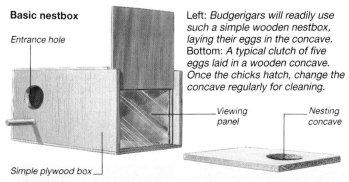

Left: *Budgerigars will readily use such a simple wooden nestbox, laying their eggs in the concave.* Bottom: *A typical clutch of five eggs laid in a wooden concave. Once the chicks hatch, change the concave regularly for cleaning.*

Viewing panel

Nesting concave

clean with a damp cloth, adult budgerigars are deprived of any opportunity to gnaw inside the box and may, therefore, resort to feather-plucking. Some breeders have also reported problems of condensation in the interior of plastic nestboxes. For these reasons, wooden concaves are still generally preferred.

Colony breeding
This is the simplest breeding system. The nestboxes are fixed in place in the aviary, under cover, and the budgerigars choose their own mates. If colony breeding is to be successful, the budgerigars must have an adequate choice of nesting sites available, which, in practical terms, means that you should provide about double the number of nestboxes to the number of pairs. Within a group of budgerigars, a distinct order of dominance will develop, so try not to have any unpaired individuals in the aviary, especially hens, which may prove very disruptive. You should refrain from adding any new budgerigars to an existing colony during the breeding period, otherwise fighting is likely to occur, and eggs and chicks may be lost. Fix the nestboxes at the same height; this will reduce the risk of fighting since the hens are likely to dispute ownership of higher boxes. You may find it easiest to secure all the nestboxes onto one long piece of wood using brackets, and then to position the complete row in the aviary. Allow sufficient space between the nestboxes so that you can inspect the interiors and clean them out easily.

Avoid the temptation to provide the budgerigars with nesting facilities before spring; breeding results tend to be better at this time, and there is less risk of complications, such as egg-binding (see page 64).

When hen birds are in top breeding condition, their ceres turn deep brown, and the birds become more destructive, shredding the paper on the floor of their quarters, for example, and gnawing intently

Above: *A dark green yellow-wing cock in prime breeding condition. Pairs normally nest readily and can breed throughout most of the year.*

extend up to just below the level of the entrance hole. This will enable you to withdraw the chicks easily from the box while ensuring that they cannot fall out. You will need a supply of concaves for each nestbox, as these will have to be changed regularly once the chicks have hatched.

Nestboxes and concaves are traditionally wooden but plastic designs are also available. Although the latter are easy to

at the perches in their aviary. Cock budgerigars in top breeding condition become more vocal, and their musical prowess is often accompanied by vertical movements of the head, which can be a prelude to mating. At this stage, the pupils contract, so that the eyes appear whitish. Cocks pursue the hen of their choice around the aviary, occasionally pausing to tap their beaks repeatedly on the perch and continuing to sing forcefully.

Budgerigars are often fickle in their breeding habits and several cocks may mate with one hen, although, generally, one particular cock remains in close attendance. When she is ready to lay, the hen spends longer periods of time in her chosen nestbox, while the cock bird may join her for some of the day and will often roost alongside his mate at night. In the immediate period prior to laying, hens often attack cuttlefish bone with relish; the calcium which it contains is vital for strong eggshells. The hen's vent area usually swells slightly when she is about to lay and her droppings will also be larger, and often have a very pungent odour; this is normal and need not cause concern.

Once the hen is settled in the nestbox, check inside each day to ensure that all is progressing well.

Above: *Hen budgerigars alone are responsible for incubating the eggs and raising the chicks until they are ready to leave the nest.*

It is a good idea to accustom the hen to this procedure before she actually lays. Gently tap on the outside of the nestbox door and give her a few moments to emerge before opening it. The egglaying period usually proceeds without problems, although in a colony aviary individual hens may prove disruptive to the breeding attempts of others, entering the nestbox and sometimes fighting viciously. Remove persistent offenders, as they can cause considerable havoc. Budgerigars typically lay a clutch of between four and six white eggs, on alternate days. The hen incubates alone, although the cock bird may keep her company for periods. She will usually start sitting in earnest only once she has laid two or three eggs. This helps to ensure that the chicks emerge closer together and that they are of a more even age when they hatch. Assuming all goes well, the eggs should start to hatch about 18 days after laying, although in the case of the first eggs this period may be slightly prolonged by the delay in the start of incubation. Newly hatched chicks have a peculiar high-pitched call, which you may be able to hear even from outside the aviary. At this stage, the chicks have a very thin covering of down over their backs and the crop is visible as a yellowish-coloured swelling that stands out very clearly when the chick has been fed.

Avoid interfering with the chicks until all the eggs are due to have hatched. Apart from those eggs which were infertile, there may be embryos that have died in the shell before hatching. Under normal circumstances, you should be able to tell whether the eggs are fertile. By 10 days into the incubation period, the developing chick and a surrounding mass of blood vessels will show up as an opacity in a fertile egg when it is viewed in a good light. Infertile eggs will show no such opacity. Checking eggs against a light source is traditionally called 'candling', a term that reflects the practice of checking poultry eggs using the light of a candle. Today, a battery torch provides the most efficient means of checking eggs for fertility. Since it is possible to see through an infertile egg, they are often described by breeders as being 'clear'. Be sure that your hands are clean and dry, before candling your budgerigars' eggs; you can contaminate the shell with bacteria, which can gain access to

the egg via the pores present in the shell and may prevent it hatching. There is no real need to candle eggs but, should the whole clutch be infertile, you can remove all the eggs in the hope that the hen will lay again in the near future.

Cage breeding
If you are interested in breeding exhibition birds, or in producing a specific colour, then cage breeding is usually recommended to ensure the parentage of the chicks. Budgerigars are fickle in their choice of mates and, in a colony system, a hen may mate with several partners in succession. It is, of course, possible to keep individual breeding pairs in small flights and the fertility of birds housed in flights is often better than that of budgerigars housed in cages. However, the cost and space required generally precludes this system of management.

You can fix the nestboxes onto the side or front of the breeding cage. It is easier to inspect a nestbox positioned at the side, but you will need to cut a hole through the part of the breeding cage to correspond to the entrance hole of

Below: *This is an ideal form of nestbox as it is easy to inspect the eggs and chicks without either falling out of the nest.*

the nestbox. You will also need to make a smaller hole for the perch. Secure the box firmly in position with a bracket.

Where space in a birdroom is at a premium, you may prefer to fix the nestboxes to the front of the breeding cage, usually in the top righthand corner. This will mean cutting away part of the mesh and you should ensure that no sharp projections remain accessible to the budgerigar; ideally, use battening to sandwich the cut ends out of reach. It is usually not practical to fix the nestboxes within the cage itself as they take up a disproportionate amount of space and can also be difficult to clean thoroughly.

When you first introduce a pair of budgerigars to the breeding cage, it is useful to close off the entrance to the nestbox for a few days to prevent the hen from retreating inside, and not emerging long enough for mating to take place. This is unlikely to be a problem in aviary surroundings, since the hens have to fly further afield in order to obtain food, and mating often occurs at this time.

Spray the adult birds with a preparation to kill red mites (*Dermanyssus gallinae*), which can become a major problem within the confines of a breeding cage. It is worth taking every precaution to prevent these parasites gaining access to the budgerigars' breeding quarters. Once established, they will multiply rapidly and can survive from one breeding season to another without feeding in the interim. They will localize in nestboxes, where they will feed on the blood of both the adult birds and their chicks. This can lead to anaemia, stunting and possibly even death.

Provided that the hen is in good condition, she should lay within about a fortnight of being given access to the nestbox. If you are concerned about the humidity in the birdroom, you can obtain a humidity gauge, (often described as a hygrometer), which will measure the relative humidity on a percentage scale. The interpretation of the resulting figure is given on the gauge i.e. in terms of 'dry' or 'humid', etc. Aim for a relative humidity of about 50%. Low humidity is most likely to be a problem in a heated environment, such as indoors in the home, or if you are breeding budgerigars during the colder part of the year in the birdroom and supplying artificial heat. You can correct dry atmosphere with a humidifier, which is basically a tray of water that evaporates by gentle heat, thus raising the humidity of the atmosphere, or by spraying around the nestbox with a plant mister, wetting the wood on the exterior.

Egg-binding
Occasionally, an egg may become stuck just above the hen's vent opening, a condition known as 'egg-binding'. Young hens nesting for the first time in cold weather are particularly vulnerable. An affected hen is likely to emerge from the nestbox at the time she is due to lay, appearing very unsteady, and will often become unable to perch within a short period of time. You will need to act quickly to save such a bird. If you examine her carefully you will probably be able to feel the egg, just above the vent area, as a relatively hard swelling. Handle the budgerigar gently to prevent the egg breaking within her body, which could lead to peritonitis (a severe infection of the body cavity). Transfer her to a warm environment, under an infrared lamp; the heat may be sufficient to encourage egg laying.

If there is no improvement within several hours, then more radical action will be necessary. You may be able to carefully manipulate the egg free, but it is advisable to contact your veterinarian without delay. Administration of calcium borogluconate may stimulate muscular contractions sufficiently to expel the egg naturally. Failing this, your veterinarian may recommend operating to save the budgerigar. It is quite possible for the bird to make a full recovery, and breed successfully afterwards, but you should wait until the following breeding season before pairing her up again.

Soft-shelled eggs are often responsible for egg-binding, so always ensure that the birds have access to cuttlefish bone. Abnormally large eggs may also cause egg-binding; sometimes these contain two yolks and if laid normally, or removed intact, and incubated successfully, may very occasionally produce twin birds.

Hatching problems

Chilling, contamination and incorrect humidity are all possible causes of hatching problems. If the hen is frightened by, perhaps, a cat or another creature at night, at some stage towards the end of the incubation period, she may leave the nest for a temporary period overnight and the eggs may be fatally chilled. Contamination of the egg shells by droppings enable

Below: *These chicks are about 6-12 days old. Budgies accept some interference when breeding, but do not disturb them unnecessarily.*

bacteria and other harmful micro-organisms to enter the egg, and this, too, can kill the embryo. Second rounds of eggs are particularly at risk when the first round chicks are still using the nestbox. Continue changing the concave so as to minimize such contamination and always wash your hands thoroughly before handling the eggs to ensure that you do not transfer bacteria to the eggs and prevent the chicks hatching as a result.

Humidity is commonly cited as a reason for deaths of chicks before hatching. In the normal process of incubation, the egg loses water. If the volume lost is inadequate, however, the chick may 'drown' inside the egg before it can free itself. Conversely, excessive water loss may cause the shell membranes to become very tough, making it harder for the chick to cut its way out of the shell.

In some instances, an egg may 'pip' (the chick makes a small hole in the shell), but hatching does not progress normally. Under these circumstances, you may decide to assist the chick out of the shell. Leave it for at least a day,

however, before taking any action, especially if blood vessels are apparent in the shell membrane, in the hope that it will free itself. There is no risk of the chick starving while it remains in the shell; the yolk-sac reserves that nourish it through the incubation period will sustain it even for a day or so after hatching.

If you do need to help the chick out of the shell then position the egg on a flat surface at a convenient height and, using a pair of tweezers, cautiously lift the shell away from the opening already made by the chick. If the membrane stuck to the shell is very tough, you may need to carefully snip it with a small pair of clean scissors. Enlarging the opening in this way, and chipping the shell with the tweezers, may be sufficient to allow the chick to free itself, provided that it is not too weak. If it has not broken out several hours later, remove more of the shell. During this process, dab the chick's navel with an iodine solution which acts as a disinfectant and dries up the exposed tissue here.

Chicks which have been helped out of the egg are not necessarily weaklings, and their subsequent development often proceeds quite normally, although obviously, losses are more likely to occur immediately after hatching.

Infertility
Recent research into the hatchability of budgerigar eggs has revealed a poor level of fertility. Only about half the eggs in the study hatched (this figure is well below that of poultry) and over three quarters of those which failed to hatch were unfertilized, rather than containing chicks which had died in their shells.

The proportion of eggs which are infertile tends to be higher in budgerigars being bred in cages. Often, this can be attributed to the incompatibility of individual pairs. Budgerigars do form significant pair bonds, and if a pair are split up from an aviary they may be

reluctant to accept new partners. For this reason, many exhibition breeders house cocks and hens in separate aviaries outside the breeding period, to prevent the formation of strong pair bonds.

The physical changes which have occurred in exhibition budgerigars may also be implicated in some cases of infertility. As with canaries, there are two recognizably distinct feather types: 'yellow' and buff. The 'yellow' form is relatively soft, whereas buff-feathered individuals have fairly coarse plumage which may obscure the vent opening of both cock and hen birds of a pair and significantly reduce the likelihood of successful mating. You may have to carefully trim the plumage here before placing the budgerigars in the breeding cage.

Egg eating
Some pairs of budgerigars acquire the unfortunate tendency to destroy their eggs as they are laid. Either the cock or hen may be responsible; you may be able to identify the culprit by the staining of the feathers around the beak with yolk. If you suspect that the cock is destroying the eggs, simply remove him from the breeding cage, allowing the hen to continue laying on her own. You may decide then to transfer the eggs to another pair that have laid at around the same time, rather than leaving the hen to rear a number of chicks on her own. In an emergency, however, she may be able to cope successfully with a few chicks. If you identify the hen as the culprit, you will need to remove the eggs for fostering, unless you can break this habit. Place one or two replacement eggs, as used by canary breeders, in the nestbox of the egg-eating pair when they have destroyed an egg. The offender will often cease this destructive behaviour, when it is unable to break the dummy egg.

In order to safeguard any eggs laid meanwhile, however, you will need to adapt the concave. Cut a hole large enough for the egg to

Concave adapted to prevent egg eating

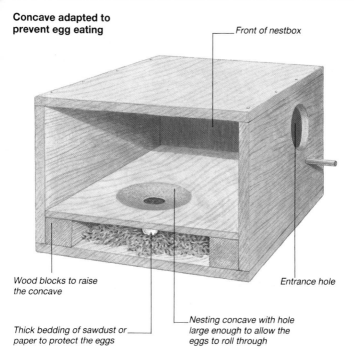

Front of nestbox

Wood blocks to raise the concave

Entrance hole

Thick bedding of sawdust or paper to protect the eggs

Nesting concave with hole large enough to allow the eggs to roll through

roll through, and then support the concave on blocks of wood at each corner so that it is raised off the floor of the nestbox. Place a thick layer of wood shavings or paper bedding (as used for hamsters) over this area, especially directly beneath the hole. When the hen lays her egg, it will roll safely through the hole on to the soft bedding beneath, out of reach. Mark the egg with a small dot using a felt-tip pen and transfer it to another pair. Most budgerigars will readily accept the eggs, and even the chicks, of other pairs and you will be able to see whether these marked eggs hatch successfully. Choose a nest with relatively few eggs, at a similar stage of development so that the chicks will hatch almost simultaneously. This should increase their chances of survival.

Occasionally, you may find that an egg has been damaged slightly in the nest. This can arise, for example, if the eggs are punctured by the overgrown claws of the parent birds. Repair minor damage

by applying nail varnish, or similar, over the area of the crack. Be sure to cover the punctured area fully, but avoid spreading the varnish too widely over the remainder of the shell's surface as this will block the pores and reduce the likelihood of successful hatching.

The rearing phase
You can offer a variety of food supplements to the adult budgerigars throughout the rearing phase (see *Feeding*, pages 43-4). It is a good idea to accustom the birds to such supplements before providing them with nesting facilities and, indeed, these may help to improve fertility if you supply them from an early age. Various softfoods, rich in protein, are available in packeted form and you should offer small amounts fresh each day. Soaked seed, particularly millet sprays, is also a popular and valuable rearing food. Simply immerse the sprays in a bowl of warm water for a day to stimulate the germination process and increase the nutritional value

of the seed. Then rinse them thoroughly under a running tap and allow to drain before feeding them to the budgerigars. You can also prepare oats or groats (the dehusked form) in this way, but avoid offering excessive amounts on a regular basis, as this can lead to obesity. Once seed has been

Above: *Check inside the beaks of the chicks as they begin to feather up and, if necessary, remove dirt using a blunt matchstick.*

soaked, you should discard it after one day before it turns mouldy. Plastic containers that hook on to the cage front or aviary mesh are

Below: *This is the first stage in fitting a young chick with a closed ring. Do not delay this task or you will be unable to fit the ring.*

Below: *You can ring chicks at just five days old. Start by grouping the three longest toes together and then slide them through the ring.*

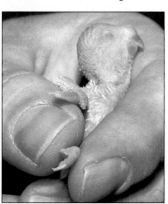

ideal for dispensing such foods, as they are easy to wash out every day. The food and water intake of the adult birds will rise as their chicks grow, and they may require larger or additional containers.

By the time the chicks are about eight days old it will be time to clean out the nestbox. While you are doing this, transfer the chicks to a spare nesting box. Remove the lid of the nestbox, change the concave and brush out the interior before replacing the chicks on a clean base. Clean the soiled concaves by immersing them in a bucket of water for several hours, and then scrubbing them thoroughly. After a good final rinse in clean water, leave them to dry in the sun or in a warm spot, such as close to a radiator.

Keep a watch on the chicks as they develop to ensure that their toes do not become encased in droppings. Some pairs of budgerigars, called 'wet feeders', have chicks which produce fairly fluid droppings, so that the interior of the nestbox soon becomes wet, and their feet easily become caked with excrement. Never attempt to pull off this dirt; you are very likely to remove a claw at the same time and ruin the exhibition prospects of the bird before it has even feathered up. Instead, fill a clean

empty yoghurt pot with tepid water and soak the foot to soften the droppings, and then cautiously chip these away with your fingernail. You should also check inside the bird's mouth for accumulations of droppings and food residue. If left, accumulated droppings or food can result in malformation of the beak, so gently prize away the obstructions using the blunt end of a matchstick.

Ringing
Assuming all goes well, the chicks grow rapidly, and can be fitted with closed rings by the time they are five days old (see page 14). This is especially important in the case of exhibition stock. You will not be able to fit such rings later in the bird's life simply because the toes will be far too big for you to slide the ring over them. Ringing is not a difficult task, but you may find it useful to have experienced help available when you first start. Gently holding the budgerigar's three longest toes together, slide the ring over to the ball of the foot. Then fold the fourth, and smallest, toe up the leg towards the knee and gently move the ring over it. Use a matchstick to ease it through the band. Once this toe is released, the ring should slide freely directly above the foot.

Below: *Fold back the small fourth toe, bringing it through the closed band of metal. A blunt matchstick is often helpful at this stage.*

Below: *Having prised this toe free, check that the ring can move freely on this part of the leg. Watch for signs of swelling later in life.*

It is particularly important to keep careful records when you have a stud of exhibition budgerigars, and it is a good idea to set up a card index, or even a computerized record, of the ring numbers, to enable you to identify all your birds and their ancestry. In addition to closed aluminium bands, you can also use split celluloid rings of various colours to distinguish between individuals in an aviary. These are more versatile as they can be fitted at any age, and their contrasting coloration means that you will be able to easily recognize budgerigars of the same plumage colour without having to catch them.

Some budgerigars react badly to the closed rings as they get older, however, and swelling around the ring can occur. If this is the case, you will need to cut off the ring to prevent the blood supply to the foot being impaired, which could result in gangrene and loss of the toes. A special tool is required to remove the ring, so as not to further damage the bird's leg. You would be well advised to seek veterinary help. In most cases the

swelling will subside without further problems once the band has been removed.

Feather-plucking
Young budgerigars begin to feather up properly by the time they are about three weeks of age. Unfortunately, the cock bird in some pairs may start to pluck the chicks just as they start to feather up, often starting around the back of the neck. The resulting devastation is often rapid; the chicks can be largely denuded even in the space of a morning, so you will need to act quickly. It is well worth having a supply of powdered aloes available for emergencies of this type. Sprinkle the powder over the plumage at the back of the neck and over the wing feathers. The bitter taste of the aloes should deter the cock bird from pulling the feathers from his offspring. Such behaviour may be stimulated in cocks by a desire to recommence nesting, feather-plucking being an attempt to drive the first round of chicks from the nest. Hens will only occasionally resort fo feather-plucking their chicks. Even if the chicks have been badly plucked, however, their appearance should improve once they fledge, and the plumage will regrow as normal.

Below: *Nest cards should be linked with a breeding and stock index. Some breeders are using computers to assist with record keeping.*

PAIR Nos	20	COCK	COLOUR	OP Grey								
SEASON	19 87		RING Nos	10 / A / 85								
DATE PAIRED	26-8-87	HEN	COLOUR	Albino								
			RING Nos	18 / A / 86								
1st ROUND	EGG Nos	1	2	3	4	5	6	7	8	9	10	
	DATE LAID	13.9.87	14/9	16/9	18/9	20/9	22/9	24/9				
	DATE HATCHED			4/10	6/10	8/10	10/10	13/10				
	RING Nos			2	3	4	5					
2nd ROUND	EGG Nos	1	2	3	4	5	6	7	8	9	10	
	DATE LAID											
	DATE HATCHED											
	RING Nos											
3rd ROUND	EGG Nos	1	2	3	4	5	6	7	8	9	10	
	DATE LAID											
	DATE HATCHED											
	RING Nos											
NOTES	Dirty feeders											

Above: *Restrict your budgerigars to two clutches of eggs in one year so as not to overburden them.*

Leaving the nest

Young budgerigars normally leave the nest by the time they are five weeks old and the cock bird will be largely responsible for feeding them until they are independent at six weeks old. In the meantime, the hen will probably be incubating her second clutch of eggs. Restrict the budgerigars to a maximum of two rounds in a breeding season so as not to overburden them. This can be harder when breeding is taking place on a colony system, and it may be necessary to transfer hens that have already raised two rounds of chicks to separate accommodation for a short period until all breeding activity has ceased. Do not merely close off nestboxes in the aviary, since there is likely to be severe squabbling over the remaining nesting sites.

Once the chicks are feeding themselves, move them to a flight cage. If you wish, you can then dispose of surplus stock as pets. However, it is very difficult to assess the likely exhibition potential of young budgerigars until after their first moult. Time spent with the young birds at this stage will be helpful in taming

them, so that they will be easier to train for exhibition purposes later in life. Remove chicks reared in the aviary on a colony system as soon as they are independent, so that they do not interfere with their parent's subsequent nesting activities. You can then return them to the aviary, along with new stock, after all the nestboxes have been removed.

The immediate post-fledging period is the time when signs of French moult are likely to become apparent (see page 14). Watch for any chicks that drop their tail and flight feathers at this stage. Although no treatment is available to cure this viral disease, you should thoroughly disinfect the nestbox, concave and surroundings to avoid the infection spreading. It appears that the virus can be transferred from one nestbox to another both by the chicks themselves and also by their droppings. Some brands of disinfectant are more suitable for use with livestock than others, functioning more effectively when there is heavy organic contamination, so seek the advice of your veterinarian. Affected budgerigars are fine as pets, but you should house them separately and, obviously, you should not use them as future breeding stock.

Budgerigar genetics

One of the fascinations of the Budgerigar is the large number of colour varieties that have been developed through the years. In a breeding aviary, however, certain colours will start to predominate over a period of time, depending on the original stock. When the budgerigars are able to mate in a haphazard fashion, it is impossible to guarantee the parentage of the resulting chicks, and breeding specific colours can be difficult. If you want to breed birds with specific colours and markings, it is essential to understand how these characteristics are passed on from one generation to another. Here, we consider the basic rules of genetics - the 'science of inheritance' – and explain some of the terms commonly used to describe the biological processes, structures and results involved. Then we look at a number of case studies that we can truly consider as examples of 'genetics in action'.

Basic rules and terms

The basic rules of genetics were first laid down by Gregor Mendel, an Austrian monk who brought the analytical eye of a mathematician to the results of exhaustive experiments he carried out, initially with pea plants. Working in the mid-1800s, Mendel recorded the inheritance of simple characteristics from one generation to another and developed a series of statistical 'rules' on the basis of the outcome. As we shall see in the examples explained below, the predicted results are most likely to be accurate over many pairings rather than in one single mating.

It was not until the early 1900s that Mendel's pioneering work and the emerging science of cell biology were harnessed into a more complete understanding of the mechanism of inheritance. Even today, when electron microscopes can probe the inner secrets of the cell, Mendel's basic 'laws' of genetics still hold true.

What Mendel knew simply as 'inherited characters' we now know exist as genes on the thread-like chromosomes within the cell nucleus. Chromosomes occur in pairs, and these become separated in the sex cells of the parents (sperm and eggs) and are recombined at conception. This splitting up and recombination process lies at the heart of genetic variation; quite simply, it allows the genetic 'cards' to be 're-shuffled' in each succeeding generation. As a result, the offspring receive genes from both their parents.

This does not mean that the offspring display a 'mixture' of their parents' characteristics. Quite the opposite, for some genes (and hence characteristics) are dominant over others and these alone may be evident in the physical appearance of the offspring. These two types of genes are called, quite simply, 'dominant' and 'recessive'.

There is an important distinction between the genetic make-up – the so-called genotype – of an individual and the outward expression of those genetic characteristics in terms of physical appearance – the phenotype – of the individual. Thus, two individuals can have the same phenotype (appearance) but different genotypes (combinations of genes).

Where two identical genes for a certain character occur opposite one another on the paired chromosomes, such as two dominant or two recessive genes, the individual is called homozygous for that character. If the genes are different, i.e. one dominant and one recessive, the individual is heterozygous, or 'split', for that character.

Just a few more words of explanation will help you to follow the case studies below. There are two kinds of chromosomes in most animal cells: one pair that determine the sex of the individual, the 'sex chromosomes', and the remaining chromosomes, the so-called 'autosomes'. In budgerigars, there are 16 pairs of chromosomes in each cell, of which 15 pairs are

Genetics at the cellular level – How sex cells are formed

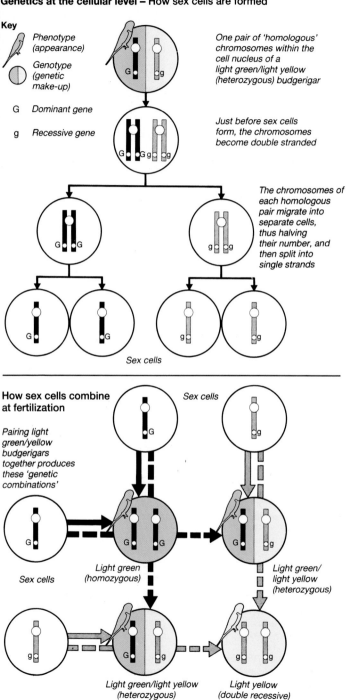

Key

Phenotype (appearance)

Genotype (genetic make-up)

G *Dominant gene*

g *Recessive gene*

One pair of 'homologous' chromosomes within the cell nucleus of a light green/light yellow (heterozygous) budgerigar

G G g g

Just before sex cells form, the chromosomes become double stranded

G G

g g

The chromosomes of each homologous pair migrate into separate cells, thus halving their number, and then split into single strands

G   G   g   g

Sex cells

How sex cells combine at fertilization

Sex cells

G   g

Pairing light green/yellow budgerigars together produces these 'genetic combinations'

G

Sex cells

G G

Light green (homozygous)

G g

Light green/ light yellow (heterozygous)

g

G g

Light green/light yellow (heterozygous)

g g

Light yellow (double recessive)

autosomes and one pair are sex chromosomes. The budgerigar's sex chromosomes are designated ZZ for male and ZY for female, with the 'Y' chromosome being shorter than the 'Z' chromosome. (This is quite different from the sex chromosomes in man, in which males have the shorter 'Y' chromosome and are designated XY; females are XX.) In the accepted notation of genetics, the first generation from a particular pairing is called the F1 generation. If those offspring are paired, the next generation is F2, and so on.

Now let us see how these genetic processes work out in a representative selection of examples.

An autosomal recessive case study

This is the commonest type of mutation, where mutant genes arise on the autosomal chromosomes rather than on the single pair of sex chromosomes. These genes are considered recessive if pairing the mutant with a light green budgerigar (dominant to all other colours) produces no mutant offspring in the first generation (F1). This supposes that both the recessive and the light green budgerigar are homozygous, i.e. with identical genes on opposing chromosomes. (In effect, 'double dominant' and 'double recessive' respectively.)

Alternatively, as we have seen, it is possible for the dominant colour to mask a gene for the recessive colour on the opposing chromosome, so that although the budgerigar in question appears light green, it is also carrying the recessive characteristic in its genetic make-up, or genotype. Thus, in this instance, its appearance (phenotype) is not the same as its genotype. Such 'split' birds cannot be distinguished from homozygous individuals except by breeding results.

In this example, the mutant colour is light yellow. Starting with a light green ('double dominant') paired with a light yellow ('double

Above: *Genetically, appearances can be deceiving; this light green budgerigar may be carrying the recessive gene for yellow.*

recessive'), all the possible pairings are shown. As you can see, if any light yellow offspring arise from mating an apparently normal (i.e. apparently 'double dominant') light green budgerigar with a light yellow budgerigar, then this confirms that the normal is 'split' for light yellow (i.e. carrying one dominant gene and one recessive gene). Furthermore, if two light green budgerigars paired together produce any light yellow offspring, they must both be 'split' for light yellow.

An autosomal recessive case study

These drawings show all the possible pairings, starting with a light green and light yellow. The letters A-E refer to the panels below, in which the tint reflects the phenotype (appearance)

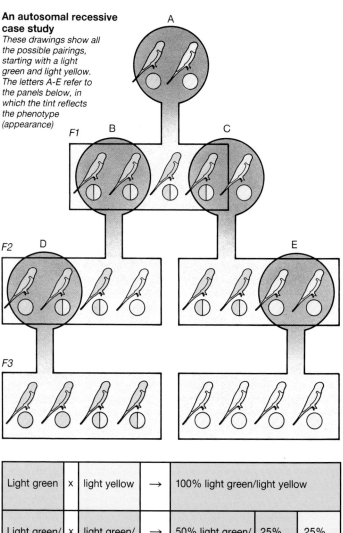

Light green	x	light yellow	→	100% light green/light yellow		
Light green/ light yellow	x	light green/ light yellow	→	50% light green/ light yellow	25% light green	25% light yellow
Light green/ light yellow	x	light yellow	→	50% light green/ light yellow	50% light yellow	
Light green	x	light green/ light yellow	→	50% light green	50% light green/ light yellow	
Light yellow	x	light yellow	→	100% light yellow		

A sex-linked recessive case study

Here, the recessive mutation affects genes located on the pair of sex chromosomes. Because the hen has sex chromosomes of different length (ZY), there will only be one gene to consider rather than two and she cannot be split for a mutation of this type, since there is no corresponding gene on the opposite, short Y chromosome. Therefore her phenotype must correspond with her genotype. In order to maximize on the number of sex-linked mutant offspring, it is vital to concentrate on keeping cocks of this colour, since, in pairings with normals, a relatively higher number of mutant chicks can be produced. The possible pairings and the results are shown opposite.

A dominant case study

In a few instances, mutations have arisen that are dominant to light green. Thus, the dominant feature can arise in the first generation, following pairing to a homozygous light green. Dominance may be either single factor (sf), if just one of the chromosomes in the pair is affected, or double factor (df), when both members of the pair carry dominant genes. It is only possible to distinguish between single and double factor individuals if normal chicks result in the first generation of a pairing to a homozygous light green; if they do, the budgerigar in question is a single-factor bird. The most recent dominant mutation to emerge is the spangle, which affects the body markings (see pages 110-111). Any budgerigars with normal markings cannot be 'split' for this characteristic, since, in effect, the normal light green characteristic is 'recessive' to the spangle feature. The results of possible pairings involving the spangle mutation are analyzed in the panel opposite.

The crested mutations

There are three different mutations of crested budgerigars, all of which are dominant in their mode of

A sex-linked recessive case study

Cinnamon cock	x	normal hen
Normal cock	x	cinnamon hen
Cinnamon cock	x	cinnamon hen
Normal/ cinnamon cock	x	normal hen
Normal/ cinnamon cock	x	cinnamon hen

A dominant case study

Spangle light green (df)	x	light green
Spangle light green (sf)	x	light green
Spangle light green (df)	x	spangle light green (df)
Spangle light green (sf)	x	spangle light green (sf)
Spangle light green (df)	x	spangle light green (sf)

inheritance, but there is also a lethal factor associated with them. This precludes the survival of double factor birds of this form. As a result, all crested budgerigars are single factor, and the standard pairing in this particular case is: Crest (sf) x normal → 50% crest (sf) + 50% normal.

Crested budgerigars are never mated together, simply because this immediately means that the anticipated 25% of double factor

50% normal/cinnamon cocks		50% cinnamon hens	
50% normal/cinnamon cocks		50% normal hens	
100% cinnamon			
25% normal cocks	25% normal/cinnamon cocks	25% normal hens	25% cinnamon hens
25% normal/cinnamon cocks	25% cinnamon cocks	25% normal hens	25% cinnamon hens

100% spangle light green (sf)		
50% spangle light green (sf)	50% light green	
100% spangle light green (df)		
50% spangle light green (sf)	25% spangle light green (df)	25% light green
50% spangle light green (df)	50% spangle light green (sf)	

birds are not viable, reducing the overall hatchability. In other respects, crested budgerigars present no difficulties in terms of their care or breeding.

Incomplete dominance
Where there is no clear dominance, it is possible to distinguish visually between single and double factor birds. This applies to the so-called dark factor, which exerts a darkening influence on the budgerigar's coloration. The presence of a single dark factor in the green series birds produces the dark green, with the double factor counterpart being described as olive green. Their respective equivalents in blue series birds are cobalt and mauve. Apart from this difference in coloration, their projected pairings are identical to those set out under the dominant case study above.

Colour varieties

In this section we look at the numerous mutations and colour forms of the budgerigar, many of which have been developed during the first half of this century. Relatively few mutations have arisen in recent years, but one, the spangle, which emerged in 1978, has attracted considerable attention among budgerigar fanciers around the world. This striking mutation affects the markings, producing an attractive dark edging around individual wing feathers, as shown in the two examples above. The first colour form to be established, also recorded in wild flocks, was the light yellow. This is now a rare variety, with breeders tending to favour the more striking lutino. In fact, a number of colours have waned in popularity, and even been lost, since the appearance of the light yellow in 1872, as others have been developed. Although there is always the possibility that these forms will re-emerge, they may not be recognized as such unless

the relevant breeding records are analyzed by a keen geneticist.

The appearance of the budgerigar has also altered quite significantly over the years; substantial birds with relatively large heads are now generally favoured. These selective changes in coloration and size have been reversed in wild birds following the release of captive-bred budgerigars. A population which originated from domestic stock has been successfully established in Florida, where flocks of free-flying budgerigars have become a tourist attraction in coastal areas. The first of these birds were released in 1956, and the population has since increased to about 3000. Natural selection has resulted in green becoming the dominant colour, since this helps to conceal their presence, and the birds have become very agile on the wing to escape predatory cats and hawks. They retain a strong flocking instinct, and nest communally, as they do in their Australian homeland.

Variations on a theme

The number of possible varieties of budgerigars is almost impossible to calculate – there are simply so many different combinations that can be produced. The figure could be in excess of one million, and this, of course, is one of the reasons for their popularity. The primary mutations, as distinct from the various combinations, can be divided into three categories: the basic colour varieties; the mutations affecting the wing markings and body patterning; and the feather variants, such as the crested forms.

How the colours are formed

Changes in coloration result from genetic alterations to the distribution of colour pigments within the feathers. A yellow pigment is normally present within the outer part of the feather. Beneath this, there is a reflective layer that creates the impression of blue coloration, although, in reality, there is no blue pigment as such. The combination of these two layers provides green coloration, just as can be achieved by mixing yellow and blue paints together. When visible yellow pigment is absent, the body coloration appears blue and the facial area becomes white.

Dark coloration is caused by the pigment melanin. When melanin is diluted – in the so-called 'cinnamon' mutation – the black markings (notably on the wings) become brown and the black eyes lighten to a plum colour.

The absence of melanin produces the bright yellow appearance of the lutino. Here even the dark mask is missing, in contrast to the light yellow, where some melanin pigment is retained. When both yellow and melanin pigments are absent, the so-called albino budgerigar results. This may have a bluish tinge in certain lights, however, because of the remaining presence of the blue layer, but there is no darker pigment.

In pied budgerigars there is a variable and sporadic absence of these pigments over the body, so they can vary widely in appearance. Changes to the blue layer occur in grey budgerigars, but it is still possible to combine yellow with a predominantly grey bird, giving rise to the aptly named yellow-faced grey mutation.

Pigmentation in the feather

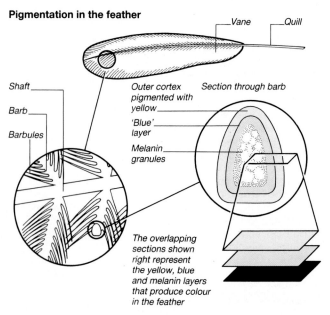

Vane

Quill

Shaft

Barb

Barbules

Outer cortex pigmented with yellow

'Blue' layer

Melanin granules

Section through barb

The overlapping sections shown right represent the yellow, blue and melanin layers that produce colour in the feather

How the colours are built up – Melanin layer represents the markings

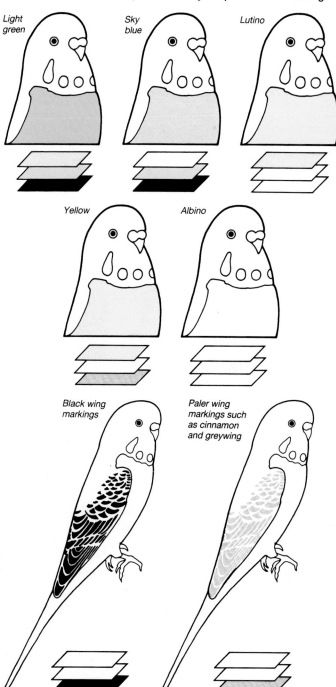

Light green

Sky blue

Lutino

Yellow

Albino

Black wing markings

Paler wing markings such as cinnamon and greywing

The colours

Green

Light green is the normal coloration of the Budgerigar. This has been so widely used in the development of other mutations that it can be difficult to obtain pure light greens. Indeed, the mating of two light green budgerigars usually gives rise to various other colours in the chicks. The emergence of the dark factor (a gene that literally 'darkens' the colour of the budgerigar) in 1915 meant that it was then possible to obtain greens of three shades: light green, dark green and olive green. Pairing dark greens together is the most versatile option in terms of colour production since, in theory, all three shades of green should be represented among the offspring.

Combining olive and yellow features has given rise to budgerigars with a body coloration of an overall mustard shade. Cere coloration is normal and the feet are greyish in colour. The popularity of some varieties has declined over recent years, and the olive yellow, now quite rare, is a good example of this trend.

Below: **Normal light green**
This is the natural colour form of the budgerigar. Wild individuals, however, tend to be much smaller than their domestic counterparts.

Above: **Normal olive green**
This colour variety represents a darkening of the normal light green shade. This particular bird is showing early signs of scaly face.

Below: **Normal dark green**
These budgies are of a laurel shade, between the light and olive green in colour. There is also a violet form of the dark green.

Grey

Two forms of grey mutation have been recorded: the recessive form, which was evolved in England, and the now widely kept Australian grey, which proved to be a dominant mutation and rapidly became established after first appearing during the 1930s. The English variety declined once the dominant greys became available in 1937, and it appears to have become extinct during the Second World War. Combining the dominant grey and light green has made it possible to evolve the grey green, which shows some similarity to an olive, although it is paler and tends to have a more even coloration.

Below: **Normal grey**
Two varieties used to exist, but it now appears that all greys are dominant. Slight differences in the depth of coloration may be noted.

Above: **Normal grey green**
Budgerigars of this colour are similar to the olive green but can be distinguished by their jet black rather than deep blue tails.

Left: **Cinnamon grey green**
Other mutations can be superimposed on changes to body coloration. The cinnamon grey green has deep brown tail feathers.

Blue

Blue budgerigars have always been popular, since the first examples were exhibited during 1910 in London. The sky blue arose just over 30 years earlier, in Belgium. The stock available to British breeders found a ready market, but because they were apparently reluctant to pair these birds with any other colour, the fertility of the blue budgerigar appears to have declined until the mid 1920s. Once the effects of the dark factor were appreciated, however, it was possible to develop cobalts (with one dark factor present) and mauves, which are darker in colour and possess two dark factors in their genetic make-up (see page 80).

At this stage, the coloration of the facial area was white. The yellow-faced characteristic did not emerge until the late 1930s, although it may well have existed

Above: **Normal cobalt**
This form is bred by combining the dark factor and blue mutations.

before this time. Two distinctive forms developed, often described as yellow-faced blue types I and II, with the former variety having lighter coloration than the latter. The deepest coloured individuals are now sometimes described as being golden-faced.

Right: **Yellow-faced cobalt**
It used to be thought impossible to combine yellow and blue on one bird, but the yellow-faced cobalt is now a popular variety.

Below: **Yellow-faced sky blue**
The yellow-faced characteristic has proved to be dominant. Originally, several different forms could be recognized.

Below left: **Normal sky blue**
Blue budgerigars have always been popular, since the sky blue mutation first appeared in a Belgian breeder's aviaries in 1882.

Above: **Yellow-faced mauve**
Mauve budgerigars, first developed in about 1924, are the blue series equivalent of the olive green; both are double dark factor.

Below: **Normal (visual) violet**
The deep violet coloration of these budgies makes them one of the most popular colour forms. They were first bred in the late 1920s.

Violet

Although this is accepted as a colour in its own right, ideally a deep purplish shade, the violet mutation is a separate dominant character. Violet budgerigars only result when this mutation is combined with both blue and dark factor characteristics. When combined with green series budgerigars, it will give rise to violet dark greens. These are distinguishable from the normal variety by their darker, and often more yellowish, coloration. Violet greens, although nowhere near as popular as the visual violet, can be of great value in improving the overall depth of coloration of violet chicks when crossed with blue series stock. Visual violet coloration can also be featured on both dominant and recessive pieds and in combination with many different forms of markings.

Lutino

This is one of the most popular colours, being an attractive rich shade of yellow, with red eyes. Its cere, beak and leg coloration match that of the albino (see page 90). Lutinos were bred on several occasions during the last century, but this mutation was not finally established until the 1930s, in the aviaries of German breeders. Although there was an autosomal recessive form of the lutino, all birds now in existence are thought to be of the sex-linked recessive variety. As the green series counterpart of the albino, lutinos may sometimes show an undesirable faint green tinge to their plumage, which is a show fault.

Below: **Lutinos**
The cere of the adult cock of this pair is purplish rather than the more normal blue. The hen's cere is the usual brownish colour.

Albino

This is the red-eyed white, which first emerged in Austria during 1931. Albino budgerigars are pure white in colour, with pink legs, reddish eyes and a pale yellowish beak. They should show as little trace of blue suffusion in their plumage as possible. Adult cocks have purplish, rather than blue, ceres; hens have brown ceres.

Exhibition albinos may still tend to be relatively small, and are less common than the lutino, which is dominant in terms of inheritance when these two mutations are paired together. The albino characteristic in budgerigars is sex-linked, although for a period there was said to be an autosomal recessive form which could

Below: **Albino**
This pure white budgerigar should show as little trace of blue as possible in its plumage.

emerge again in the future. (See *Budgerigar genetics*, pages 72-7, for clarification of these terms.)

White

This mutation, white with black eyes, has a similar history to that of the lutino (see page 89), but did not emerge until 1920. It is smaller than its yellow counterparts and has never achieved the same degree of popularity.

Yellow

The black-eyed variety of the yellow was certainly in existence before the end of the last century, but has faded rather in popularity with the rise of the lutino. Such birds can be easily distinguished by their black eyes and dark feet, as well as the normal blue cere of the cock birds. Throat spots are absent, with the coloration of the cheek patches being mauve, rather than white, as in a lutino.

Dark-eyed clears

These 'clear' yellow or 'clear' white budgerigars originated in Europe towards the end of the 1940s, and were first described as lutinos and albinos with black eyes. This information proved incorrect, however, since they had plum-coloured eyes, reflecting the role of the Danish recessive pied in their ancestry. It is possible to breed dark-eyed clears by pairing these pieds with dominant continental clear-flights (see page 99) in the first generation, then mating the clear-flighted offspring back to the recessive pieds. These birds have not become very popular, partly because it has proved difficult to increase their size because of the Danish recessive pied stock used in their development.

Below: **Dark-eyed clear yellow**
These budgerigars, developed using Danish recessive pieds, are distinguishable from the lutino by their plum rather than red eyes.

Pied (dominant)

Pied budgerigars show a combination of coloured and clear areas in their plumage, and it is possible to distinguish between dominant and recessive forms visually as well as genetically. The Australian dominant pied was first bred near Sydney in 1935, and became available in Europe during the late 1950s. These birds resembled normals, in terms of their black eye coloration and white irises, with throat spots and cheek flashes being present. In some cases, the clear area of plumage forms a distinctive band across the front of the body, with the wings also being clear from this point downwards. These birds are described as banded pieds, in contrast to those in which the patterning is more random.

As a dominant mutation, these pieds rapidly increased in numbers, but crossings with the Danish recessive pied left an indelible mark, which has still not been fully eliminated even today. These crossings have affected the head markings, specifically the mask, with the loss of throat spots and some variation in cere coloration also being apparent.

Below: **Grey green dominant pied**
Pied budgerigars may be 'banded', with an even clear band around the body, or, as here, may show larger areas of clear plumage.

Right: **Sky blue dominant pied**
*Any shade of blue coloration can
be offset against areas of white
plumage. Yellow-faced blue and
grey pieds can also be bred.*

Below: **Dark green dominant pied**
*Green of any shade can be
combined with yellow. The extent
of the pied markings can be quite
variable, even between nestmates.*

Pied (recessive)

This mutation had arisen by 1932, when a pied budgerigar of this variety was exhibited at a show in Copenhagen, Denmark. As a result, they became known as Danish recessive pieds. Being an autosomal recessive mutation, breeders at first tended to pair their birds together rather than outcrossing them to normals, the latter yielding no pied offspring in the first generation. Danish recessive pieds were much more slender than their dominant counterparts, and this trend is still apparent today.

They have plum-coloured eyes with no apparent irises, even when adult, and cocks have purplish-mauve, rather than blue, ceres. The number of spots present in the mask is a variable feature. They can be bred in the full range of colours, including dark factor combinations, such as the olive green recessive pied, where the clear yellow body plumage and darker markings are offset against olive green areas.

Below: **Dark green recessive pied**
These pieds can be bred in all the usual colour combinations. They tend to be more nervous than their dominant counterparts.

Above: **Grey green recessive pied**
The wings should be mainly free from black markings in these pieds, ideally extending over less than 20 percent of the wing area.

Below: **Cobalt recessive pied**
The number of throat spots present in these recessive pieds is a variable feature, ranging from one to a full complement of six.

Cinnamon

This mutation is a sex-linked recessive characteristic and first arose in 1931. It alters the markings, causing them to be brown, rather than black, and the eye coloration becomes a deep shade of plum red. Although at first known as the cinnamonwing, this became shortened just to cinnamon. This feature can be combined with both blue and green series birds. Various forms of the cinnamon mutation have arisen in different parts of the world, from Australia to the United States of America.

The characteristic plum-coloured eyes can be seen in chicks as soon as they hatch and using this facet of the cinnamon mutation can be a very valuable way of sexing the chicks of certain pairings. Pairing a cinnamon cock with a normal hen is a good example, since the cinnamons (i.e. with plum-coloured eyes) in the resulting nest must be hens and all the remaining birds must be cocks.

Below: **Cinnamon light green**
The cinnamon mutation reduces the concentration of melanin, changing black markings to brown.

Above: **Cinnamon sky blue**
The modified wing and tail coloration, with the characteristic brown tinge, is clearly shown here.

Left:
Cinnamon yellow-faced sky blue
Note the cinnamon-brown throat spots, matching the wing markings.

Above: **Opaline cinnamon grey**
*It has proved possible to combine
more than one mutation affecting
the wing markings on a single bird,
as shown by this example.*

Right: **Opaline cinnamon yellow-
faced grey**
*An attractive colour combination,
underlining the wide diversity of
varieties that can now be bred.*

Pied (clear-flighted)

In this variety the flight feathers are clear (i.e. yellow in green series and white in blue series birds). There appear to be distinctive continental and Australian strains, but they are not especially popular.

Below: **Clear-flighted sky blue dominant pied**
Clear-flights of all the normal colours can be bred. Green series birds have yellow flight and tail feathers, whereas those of blue or grey budgies are white, as here.

Greywing

As their name suggests, here the black markings of the normal budgerigar are diluted to grey, with the body coloration tending to be relatively unaffected. It is possible that this mutation may have arisen as long ago as 1918.

Right: **Greywing sky blue**
In this mutation, the black markings on the wings and body are reduced to grey, and the body coloration is also lightened.

Below: **Greywing light green** (left) and **greywing cobalt** (right)
The overall coloration of these budgerigars is paler than normal. The greywing light green was first bred in 1925, when it was known as the apple green. The blue form appeared three years later.

Whitewing

A member of the so-called clearwing group, this mutation alters the coloration on the wings, so that they become virtually white, with very little trace of melanin apparent. By combining the yellow-face characteristic with opaline and clearwing features, it has proved possible to produce the striking and much sought-after rainbow budgerigar.

Below: **Whitewing sky blue**
The wing markings of the whitewing are paler than those of the greywing. The body coloration is that of the normal sky blue.

Yellow-wing

Here, the yellow wing markings (virtually free of melanin) create an attractive contrast with the green body coloration, especially in dark factor birds. This mutation can also be combined with the opaline characteristic, yielding opaline yellow-wing dark greens and other colours. The yellow-wing characteristic is recessive to the ordinary green, so all offspring from a pairing of this kind will be split for the yellow-wing markings (i.e. they appear light green but carry the recessive gene for yellow-wing). Yellow-wing budgerigars will be produced if these chicks in turn are paired with yellow-wing stock.

As with mating green and blue budgerigars together, so the yellow-wing mutation is dominant to the whitewing, with all offspring of a yellow-wing x whitewing pairing being yellow-wing/ whitewing (split).

Below: **Dark green dominant pied**
Appearances can be deceptive: although it has yellow wings, this bird is a pied, and not a yellow-wing; compare the wing markings.

Above: **Yellow-wing light green**
This is a young cock bird. Pairing yellow-wings with whitewings can improve their coloration. Both are known as clearwings.

Lacewing

This is one of the few budgerigar mutations to have emerged since the Second World War. The lacewing has proved to be a sex-linked characteristic affecting red-eyed budgerigars, creating a lace-like pattern of pale brown markings on their wings, with throat spots and coloured cheek patches also being present. Lacewings are not presently among the most common varieties. Although at first they were believed to be the result of the introduction of cinnamon blood, this has now been disproved and lacewings are accepted as a separate variety.

Below: **Lacewing yellow** (left) **yellow-wing dark green** (right) *The yellow-wing characteristic can be combined with any shade of green; this variety is one of the most striking. The attractive lacewing was first bred in 1946.*

Opaline

This pattern of markings is very common, with the mutation arising in both Australia and Europe during the early 1930s. In opalines the barring on the head is less prominent, and in a well-marked individual there is a V-shaped area on the back free of markings. The darker plumage is thus confined solely to the wings and does not extend from the base of the neck downwards, as is the case in normally marked budgerigars.

The appearance of some opalines is spoilt by the presence of excess barring or flecking on the forehead, which should be clear.

Below: **Opaline dark green**
The three original forms of the opaline mutation all appeared in the early 1930s, in Scotland, Belgium and Australia.

This fault is most commonly seen in grey budgerigars, with or without yellow faces, but can be encountered in other colour varieties as well.

The opaline is a sex-linked characteristic and can be combined with many other mutations, even pieds. In this case, the markings may be further broken down, most noticeably over the wings.

Top: **Opaline (visual) violet**
Scottish opalines often show an excess of barring, especially at the back of the neck, where a clear V-shaped area is desirable.

Bottom:
Opaline yellow-faced cobalt
The opaline characteristic can be combined with any colour. It is often difficult to produce opalines with the clear V shape, however.

Above: **Opaline yellow-faced sky blue dominant pied**
The normally white areas of plumage have a pale lemon coloration on this cock budgerigar. This is a feature shared with all yellow-faced blue pied mutations. Note the less prominent barring on the head of both this bird and the opaline sky blue dominant pied.

Right:
Opaline sky blue dominant pied
Even when combined with a dominant mutation, the opaline markings still remain a sex-linked recessive feature (see Budgerigar genetics, page 76, for explanation of these genetic terms).

Fallow

Green series fallows can be especially striking in coloration, with their dark red eyes and golden yellow body plumage contrasting with greenish brown markings and throat spots. Three different forms of this mutation are known to have occurred, firstly in the United States during 1931. This line appears not to have been established, however, and it is the German strain which is best known. These budgerigars were bred at about the same time as those in the United States, and descriptions suggest that they were similar in appearance.

Slightly later, in 1933, the Australian fallow mutation was reported for the first time. Since then, however, fallows have tended to decline in numbers in Europe, although they are still common in Australia.

Overleaf: **Cinnamon English fallow light green** (top) **cinnamon English fallow sky blue** (bottom)

Below: **German fallow sky blue**
English and German fallows are now better known than other fallow varieties. The German form can be distinguished from the English by the iris around each eye.

Above: **English fallow light green**
Left: **English fallow dark green**
*The distinction between these
English fallows and the German
form (page 107) is seen in the eyes.*

Spangle

One of the latest budgerigar mutations to be recorded, the spangle has become very widely known since it was first reported from the state of Victoria, Australia in 1977. This mutation has a rather similar effect to that of the pearl recognized in cockatiels. The plumage over the wings is light in the centre, with attractive dark edging around the individual feathers, although the depth of the markings vary, depending on the bird. The flight feathers and tail are similarly marked and the throat spots have pale centres.

As a dominant mutation, it has proved possible to build up the number of spangle budgerigars rapidly. Dark factor spangles tend to be most impressive in terms of their markings.

Single and double factor birds can be distinguished visually in this case, with the markings being less evident in the latter case.

Below: **Spangle Grey**
There are two forms of the spangle. This is an example of the darkly marked single factor type.

Above: **Spangle mauve** (top) and **spangle cobalt** (bottom)
The spangle has been combined with many different colours. This was made easier because the original stock proved to be highly fertile. Double factor birds have very pale markings on their wings.

Left: **Spangle sky blue**
The pairing of double factor spangles in breeding programmes often seems to result in strongly marked single factor offspring.

Feather variants

Crested

Three distinctive forms of crested budgerigar can be produced. The full-circular has an even crest positioned centrally on the head, reaching down to, but not obscuring, the eyes or the cere. The effect resembles that of a Corona Gloster Canary. The half-circular is similar in appearance, but the crest extends only forwards from a point above the eyes towards the beak. The third form of crest is the tufted, where the plumage above the cere is raised to form a tuft.

Although crested budgerigars have been known since the 1920s in Australia, there has been relatively little interest shown in them and they remain quite scarce. Nevertheless, these crested characteristics can be combined with any chosen colour or variety, which offers considerable scope for the dedicated breeder. As explained on page 76, crested budgerigars should not be paired together, but with normal stock.

Above:
Half-circular crested sky blue
One of three distinctive types of crest recognized in budgerigars.

Below:
Full-circular crested opaline
An even, well-positioned crest is required in this, the rarest, form.

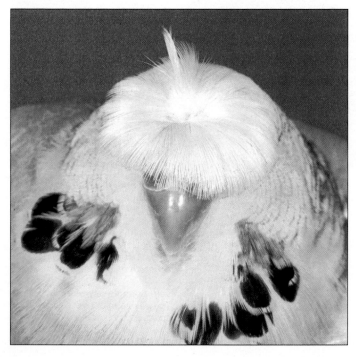

Above: **Tufted grey green**
Tufted budgerigars, first bred in Australia, are the most common form of the crested varieties. The tuft should be well shaped.

Long-flighted

The flight feathers of such budgerigars are greatly elongated, and those from each wing actually cross each other. Although these birds were soon banned from the show bench, they left a lasting impression, with their large heads acting as a stimulus to breeders. A large head is now considered very important in exhibition stock, as changes to the official standard during recent decades have revealed. Whether this trait is desirable in terms of the budgerigar's overall appearance is another matter. Certainly, the leading show birds of today are further removed in terms of appearance from wild budgerigars than the winning budgerigars of 30 years ago. Increasing problems with fertility, however, may yet cause a rethink in what constitutes the 'ideal' budgerigar.

Right: **Long-flighted opaline grey dominant pied**
The flight feathers of this variety are abnormally long, causing them to overlap. These birds are not popular and are now quite rare.

Rare varieties

Not all colour mutations which have appeared have been established successfully. Some of these could re-emerge in the future. As an example, a brownwing budgerigar was bred in Australia in the late 1980s, with chocolate-brown wing markings and deep plum-red eyes. A similar mutation had been recorded in the UK in the late 1940s, but then died out.

An interesting variety that crops up occasionally, but has not been established, is the bicolour or 'half-sides' budgerigar. It is not a mutation, merely a freak, possibly resulting from double fertilization of one egg. In these birds there is an obvious division down the centre of the body, with different colours on either side. A budgerigar of this type was first shown in 1929 in the UK. It was green on one half of its body and blue on the other. Even more unusual was a tricoloured hen,

exhibited six years later. This was blue and green as before, but had a yellow face. Various explanations have been put forward to account for the striking appearance of these birds, and all agree that these markings are not an inherited characteristic.

Not all colours can be bred, and indeed, in spite of a large cash offer by a seed supplier to the first breeder of a pink budgerigar, this prize seems likely to go unclaimed. Nevertheless, in theory at least, it may be possible to create a black budgerigar, adding at some stage in the future to the already extensive choice of varieties presently available.

Below: **Japanese heavenly body**
This opaline sky blue hen displays abnormal tufted feathering on its back and wings as well as on its head. Such budgerigars are neither common nor very popular.

Feather-dusters

These individuals are not recognized as a variety, but crop up from time to time. They often appear very promising as nestlings, frequently developing faster then their companions, but it soon becomes apparent that their plumage will not stop growing. It can reach the point where they are unable to see, and their feathering needs to be trimmed back if they are to find their food. As a general rule, feather-dusters are shortlived, rarely surviving for more than a year, and cannot fly. The cause of the condition is unclear. It may be genetic in origin, leading to disturbances in the functioning of the thyroid gland or growth hormone output within the body. Although thankfully not yet very common, the signs seem to be that the numbers of feather-dusters being bred are increasing, and modifications to the breeding programme are recommended under these circumstances.

Below: **Feather-dusters**
Another abnormality affecting the plumage. The feathers of such budgerigars grow excessively, and the birds do not live long.

Index to colour varieties

Page numbers in **bold** indicate major references, including accompanying photographs. Page numbers in *italics* indicate captions to other illustrations. Less important text entries are shown in normal type.

Picture credits

Artists
Copyright of the artwork illustrations on the pages following the artists' names is the property of Salamander Books Ltd.

John Francis: 19, 22-3, 25, 26-7, 30-1, 32, 36-7

Alan Harris: 51

Maltings Partnership: 60

David Noble: 73, 75, 80, 81

Guy Troughton: 42, 47, 67

Photographs
Unless otherwise stated, all the photographs have been taken by and are the copyright of Cyril Laubscher. The publishers wish to thank the following photographers who have supplied other photographs for this book. The photographs have been credited by page number.

Ian Hunt: © Salamander Books 40-1, 45

Ideas into Print: 53 (D. Brown), 68 (D. Brown)

Acknowledgements

The publishers wish to thank the following for their help in preparing this book: Ghalib Al-Nasser, Ash Green Village Petshop, Brian Byles, Mick and Marion Cripps, Joan Denton, Bruce and Margaret Duthie, Ray Fowler, Kevin Fraser, Simon Gage, Stanley Maughan, Ron Oxley, Sue and Trevor Phillips, John Plommer, Horry Porter, Porter's Cage Bird Appliances, Colin Putt, Dave and Sandra Rowe, Fred Sherman, Ernie Sigston, Brian Spendley, Steve Stephenson, Alan Tinham, Cliff Wright, Margaret Young

Further reading

Alderton, D. *Looking after Cage Birds* Ward Lock, 1982, 1987
Alderton, D. *A Birdkeeper's Guide to Pet Birds* Salamander Books, 1987
Alderton, D. *The Complete Cage and Aviary Bird Handbook* Pelham Books, 1986
Elliott, F.S. & Brooks, E.W. *Budgerigar Matings and Colour Expectations* The Budgerigar Society, 1984
Harper, D. *Pet Birds for Home and Garden* Salamander Books, 1986
Howson, E. *The Book of the Budgerigar* Saiga Publishing, 1981
Rogers, C.H. *The World of Budgerigars* Saiga Publishing, 1981
Rutgers, A. *Budgerigars in Colour* Blandford Press, 1967
Scoble, J. *The Complete Book of Budgerigars* Blandford Press, 1982
Taylor, T.G. & Warner, C. *Genetics for Budgerigar Breeders* The Budgerigar Society, 1986

Cinnamon grey green